BRITISH RAILWAYS

PAST and PRESENT

Special

THE SEVERN VALLEY RAILWAY

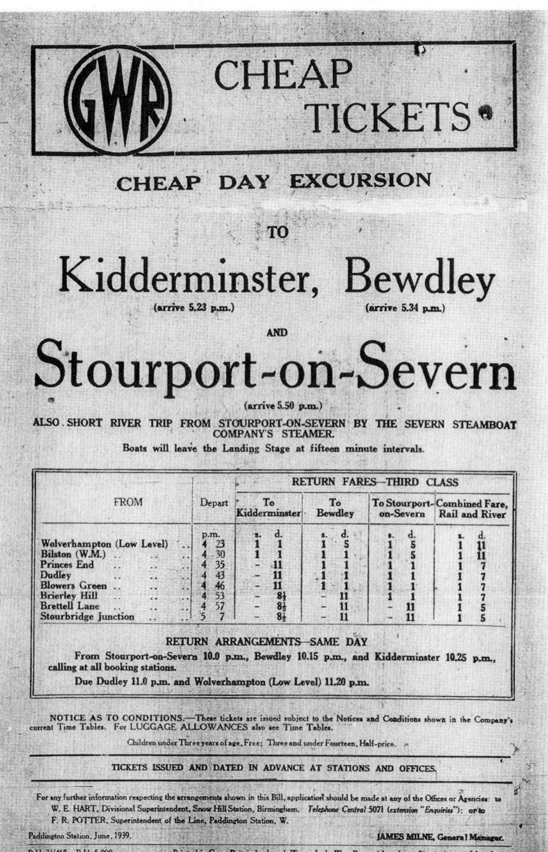

GWR CHEAP TICKETS

CHEAP DAY EXCURSION

TO

Kidderminster (arrive 5.23 p.m.), Bewdley (arrive 5.34 p.m.)

AND

Stourport-on-Severn

(arrive 5.50 p.m.)

ALSO SHORT RIVER TRIP FROM STOURPORT-ON-SEVERN BY THE SEVERN STEAMBOAT COMPANY'S STEAMER.

Boats will leave the Landing Stage at fifteen minute intervals.

FROM	Depart		RETURN FARES—THIRD CLASS							
			To Kidderminster		To Bewdley		To Stourport-on-Severn		Combined Fare, Rail and River	
	p.m.		s.	d.	s.	d.	s.	d.	s.	d.
Wolverhampton (Low Level) ..	4	23	1	1	1	5	1	5	1	11
Bilston (W.M.)	4	30	1	1	1	1	1	5	1	11
Princes End	4	35	-	11	1	1	1	1	1	7
Dudley	4	43	-	11	1	1	1	1	1	7
Blowers Green	4	46	-	11	1	1	1	1	1	7
Brierley Hill	4	53	-	8½	-	11	1	1	1	7
Brettell Lane	4	57	-	8½	-	11	-	11	1	5
Stourbridge Junction	5	7	-	8½	-	11	-	11	1	5

RETURN ARRANGEMENTS—SAME DAY

From Stourport-on-Severn 10.0 p.m., Bewdley 10.15 p.m., and Kidderminster 10.25 p.m., calling at all booking stations.

Due Dudley 11.0 p.m. and Wolverhampton (Low Level) 11.20 p.m.

NOTICE AS TO CONDITIONS.—These tickets are issued subject to the Notices and Conditions shown in the Company's current Time Tables. For LUGGAGE ALLOWANCES also see Time Tables.

Children under Three years of age, Free; Three and under Fourteen, Half-price.

TICKETS ISSUED AND DATED IN ADVANCE AT STATIONS AND OFFICES.

For any further information respecting the arrangements shown in this Bill, application should be made at any of the Offices or Agencies: to W. E. HART, Divisional Superintendent, Snow Hill Station, Birmingham. *Telephone Central* 5071 (*extension "Enquiries"*): or to F. R. POTTER, Superintendent of the Line, Paddington Station, W.

Paddington Station, June, 1939. JAMES MILNE, General Manager.

B.H. 31/468 B.H. 5,000. Printed in Great Britain by Joseph Wones Ltd., West Bromwich; also at Birmingham and London.

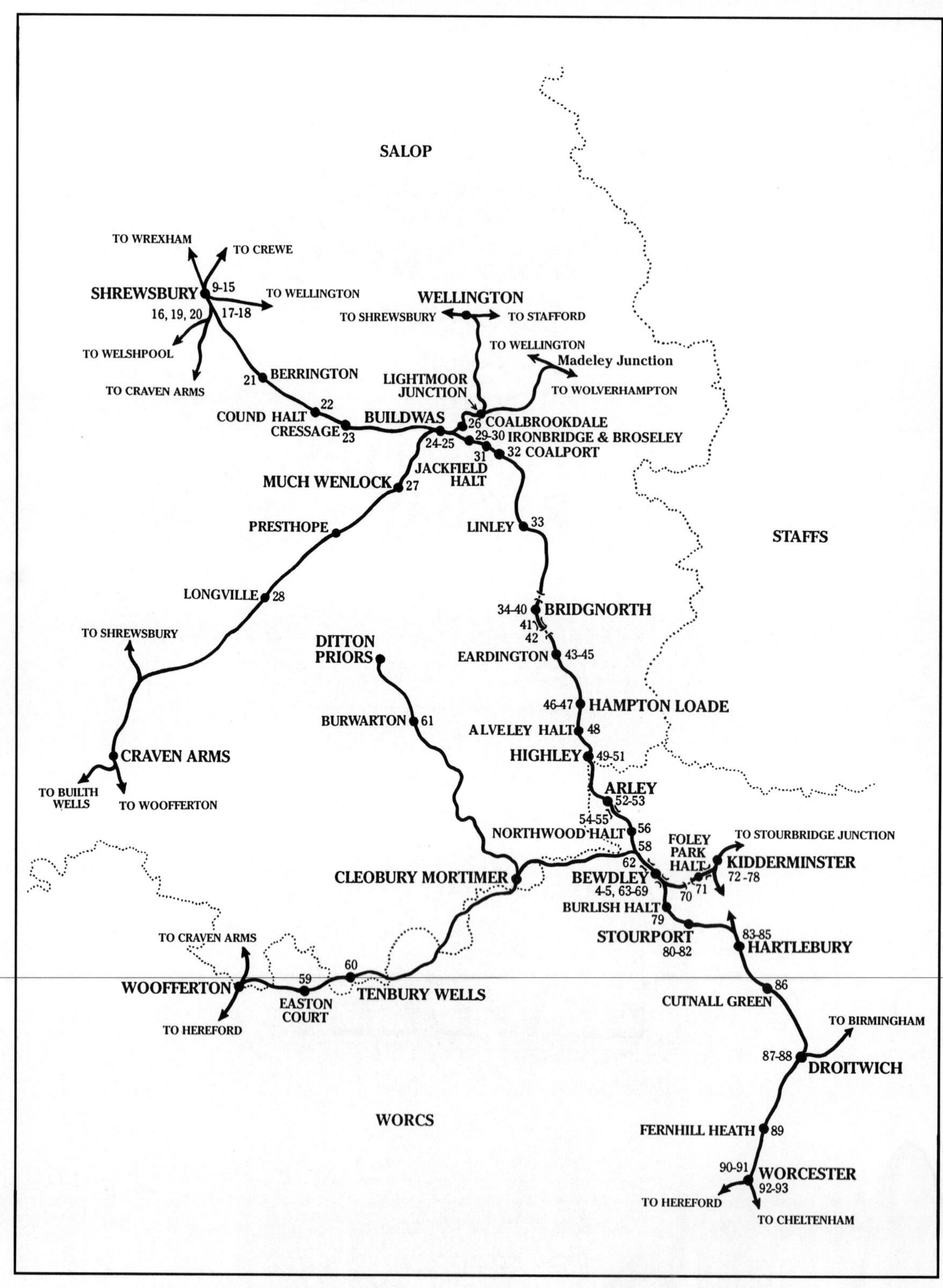

Map of the Severn Valley Railway and branches from Shrewsbury to Worcester.
The numbers refer to the page numbers where photographs of each location may be found.

A nostalgic trip along the whole route from Shrewsbury to Worcester

Roger Siviter ARPS

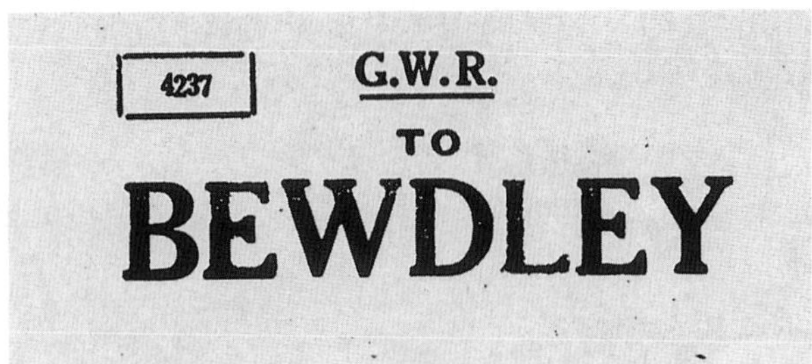

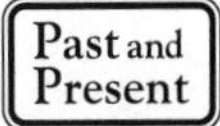

Past & Present Publishing Ltd

First published in April 1995

British Library Cataloguing in Publication Data

A catalogue record for this book is available from the British Library.

ISBN 1 85895 080 5

Past & Present Publishing Ltd
Unit 5
Home Farm Close
Church Street
Wadenhoe
Peterborough PE8 5TE
Tel/fax (01832) 720440

Maps, layout plans and gradient profiles drawn by Christina Siviter

Tickets and other items of ephemera are from the collection of Raymond Franks, and the timetables from Brian Moone

Printed and bound in Great Britain

Below and right **Bewdley station on 30 June 1966, as ex-LMS '8F' 2-8-0 No 48531 trundles through with a load of coal from Alveley Colliery bound for Stourport Power Station. Although the line between Shrewsbury and Bewdley was closed to passengers from 9 September 1963, the passenger service from Bewdley to Kidderminster and Birmingham, and also to Hartlebury and Worcester, continued until January 1970, which would account for the tidiness of the station.**

The same scene 28 years later, on 1 August 1994, shows Class '2MT' 2-6-0 No 46521 (an LMS-type locomotive, but built by British Railways at Swindon) arriving at Bewdley with the 2.45 pm from Bridgnorth to Kidderminster. Apart from lamps, signs, etc, outwardly very little seems to have changed. The main change is that Bewdley is now the headquarters of the Severn Valley Railway, so the administration offices are located there, both in the station building itself and in the extra office accommodation that has been added in the station grounds. *Both RS*

CONTENTS

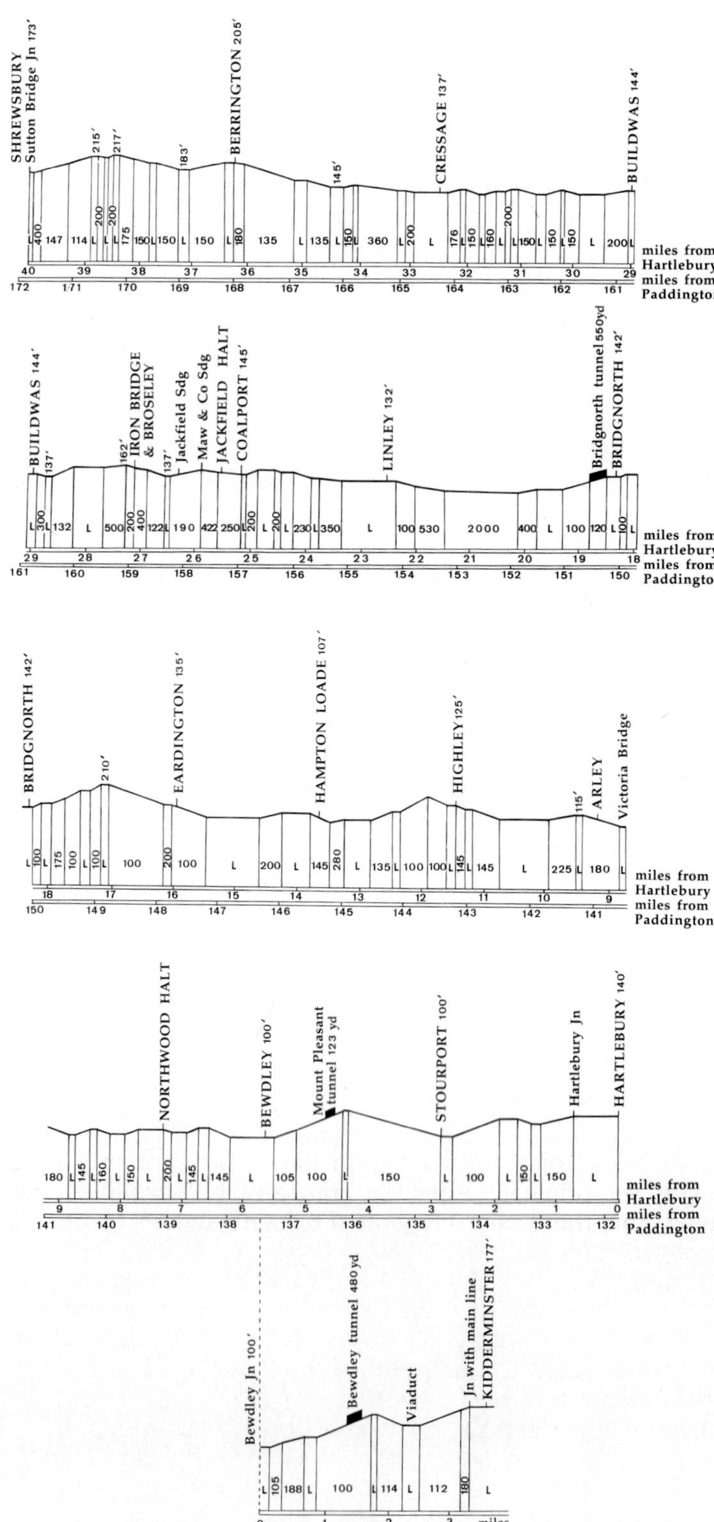

Gradient profiles of the line

INTRODUCTION

Although today many people think of the Severn Valley Railway (SVR) as being that between Kidderminster, Bewdley and Bridgnorth, this in fact only represents a section of the original line from Shrewsbury to Worcester, with Kidderminster being a branch line from Bewdley. This was, however, a most important branch, connecting Birmingham and the Black Country with the riverside towns of Stourport and Bewdley, popular with day-trippers and holidaymakers. The connection with Kidderminster also provided a through route to the industrial West Midlands and beyond for coal and freight traffic.

The line, which opened in 1862, was single throughout the 39½ miles from Shrewsbury to Hartlebury, the other 12 miles to Worcester being part of the former West Midland Railway (originally the Oxford-Worcester-Wolverhampton section), as was the Severn Valley Railway. All these lines were absorbed into the Great Western in 1863.

The Bewdley-Kidderminster loop, some 5½ miles in length, was completed in 1878. It had been hoped to complete this section in 1865, but the long delay was caused mainly by financial constraints, which affected the GWR along with other railway companies throughout the 1860s, together with wrangling with the LNWR over alternative routes, and the Staffordshire & Worcestershire Canal Company, who saw the line as a threat to themselves.

The line followed the course of the River Severn from Hartlebury to Shrewsbury, and in consequence it was free of severe gradients. After leaving Hartlebury it immediately swung westwards to Stourport, some 3 miles away, where a network of canals and the River Stour connected with the River Severn. After Stourport, the line ran in a roughly north-westerly direction through Burlish Halt, then just south of Bewdley the line from Kidderminster was encountered, and the two routes ran parallel into Bewdley station.

A mile after leaving Bewdley, the branch to Tenbury headed westwards, crossing the Severn immediately after the junction. This line was opened in 1864 and joined up with the line from Woofferton to Tenbury, opened in 1861. This lasted until 1965, when the last section of the 15½ miles from Bewdley to Tenbury, that between Cleobury Mortimer and Bewdley, was completely closed, as was the 5¼-mile line fro Woofferton to Tenbury.

From Cleobury Mortimer ran the famous Cleobury Mortimer & Ditton Priors Light Railway (CM&DP), 12 miles long and running in a north-westerly direction between the two named places. At Ditton Priors there was a rope-worked incline from the quarry at Brown Clee Hill. Although the Light Railway Order was granted in 1901, it was not until 1908 that a goods service started. The line was originally a private company, but was absorbed into the GWR in 1922, then taken over from the Western Region of British Railways by the Admiralty in 1957. It had closed to passenger traffic in 1938, and closed completely in 1965.

Back on the SVR, the line closely followed the River Severn through Northwood Halt and Arley (where just south of the station it crossed the river). It then went on to Highley, where there were connections with the local colliery and others in the nearby coalfield. After Highley the line passed through Hampton Loade and Eardington before arriving at the major Shropshire town of Bridgnorth, some 18¼ miles from Hartlebury. Today this is, of course, the northern terminus of the preserved SVR, 16 miles from Kidderminster.

After leaving Bridgnorth the line passed through Linley Halt before reaching the next major station at Coalport, famous for its pottery, where on the eastern side of the River Severn was the terminus of the LNWR branch from Wellington. The line then ran through the Severn Gorge and, after passing through Jackfield Halt, entered the station of Ironbridge & Broseley, some 2 miles from Coalport. The Ironbridge area is the home of the Industrial Revolution, where the first cast-iron bridge was built in 1777, now happily preserved. Also at Ironbridge is a museum, which together with the famous bridge now forms a considerable attraction for visitors from all over the world.

After Ironbridge the line reached Buildwas, which was the junction for Wellington to the north-east, and to Much Wenlock and Craven Arms to the west. The line to Wellington was completed in 1864, and that to Craven Arms in 1867, thus forming a through route to the Shrewsbury-Hereford and South Wales line. The line from Coalbrookdale and Wellington entered Buildwas south of the station via the Albert Edward Bridge across the Severn. The line from Madeley Junction on the Shrewsbury-Wolverhampton line, which met the Wellington line at Lightmoor Junction, is still in use today to serve Ironbridge (Buildwas) Power Station.

From Buildwas to Shrewsbury, just over 12 miles, the SVR ran through the pleasant pastoral plain of southern Shropshire, passing through Cressage, Cound Halt and Berrington, and joining the main Shrewsbury-Hereford line at Sutton Bridge Junction.

The line from Shrewsbury to Bewdley was closed for passenger traffic on 9 September 1963, and from Bewdley to Hartlebury and Kidderminster on 5 January 1970. By that time all goods (coal) traffic had ceased, with the exception of Stourport CEGB Power Station to Hartlebury, which closed in 1980, and Kidderminster to Foley Park (for the sugar works), which also ended in 1980.

The Severn Valley Railway preservation group was formed in 1965, and the line was reopened as follows:

23 May 1970: Bridgnorth-Hampton Loade
12 April 1974: Hampton Loade-Highley
18 May 1974: Highley-Bewdley
30 July 1984: Bewdley-Kidderminster (SVR)

On 12 December 1984 the junction with BR at Kidderminster was passed, and the first through working between the two systems took place on 29 December of that year, a magnificent tribute to all the enthusiasts who have made it such a superb line, not only to see, but also to travel on.

I should like to thank the following people for their help in compiling this book, without whom it would not have been possible: the Management and Staff of the Severn Valley Railway; Keith Davies and the Shropshire Railway Society; Geoff Bannister, Brian Moone, John Tennant and Barrie Geens; Wayne Massey, Shrewsbury Station Manager; all the individual photographers credited herein, and Lens of Sutton; and my wife Christina, for the maps, layout plans, typing, etc.

Roger Siviter ARPS
Bromsgrove

BIBLIOGRAPHY

Bannister, G. F. *Branch Line Byways, Vol 1: The West Midlands* (Atlantic Transport Publishers)
Christiansen, Rex *Forgotten Railways, Vol 2: Severn Valley and Welsh Border* (David & Charles)
Geens, Barrie *The Severn Valley Railway at Arley* (Wild Swan Publications Ltd)
Marshall, John *The Severn Valley Railway* (David St John Thomas)
Williams, D. C. *Severn Valley Railway Souvenir Guide* (Severn Valley Railway Company)

1
SHREWSBURY

On 4 June 1962 ex-GWR Class '4MT' 2-6-2T No 5555 prepares to depart from platform 6 with a Severn Valley line train to Worcester. The overall roof that spanned the southern half of the station was demolished in the summer of 1963.

On 6 August 1994 Class '150' unit No 150132 is seen at platform 6 with the 09.52 from Pwllheli going forward as the 13.18 to Birmingham New Street. Canopies have replaced the overall roof and side screens, but the station buildings and the footbridge, which connects the eastern side of the station with the main entrance and town centre, is still there. The dereliction in the background is a reminder of more prosperous times. *John Tennant/RS*

Ex-LMS Class '5MT' 4-6-0 No 45143 waits at platform 7 on Saturday 5 August 1961 with a southbound extra. This scene gives a closer view of the screen that enclosed the platform areas. The outer lines, used mainly by through goods traffic, can be seen below the screen. Also worthy of note are the footplatemen's uniforms and hats.

The same scene 33 years later sees Class '158' No 158815 leaving platform 7 with the 11.33 Manchester Piccadilly to Cardiff Central service on 6 August 1994. The overall roof, which disappeared in 1963, has long been replaced with separate umbrella-type platform canopies, but the outer running lines are still there, although the one by the disused platform looks as though it is not used very often. *Michael Mensing/RS*

A glance at the next two pictures, taken some 28 years apart, shows that except for the motive power and stock very little seems to have changed at Shrewsbury station. The 'past' view, taken on 25 October 1966, shows BR Standard Class '4MT' 4-6-0 No 75016 about to depart from platform 4 with the down 'Cambrian Coast Express' for Aberystwyth and Pwllheli, the train splitting at Machynlleth. This train, which originated at Paddington, continued with steam haulage until March 1967, when through workings from Paddington to Birkenhead came to an end.

The second view, taken on 6 August 1994, shows a modern-day Cambrian Coast train with Class '156' 'Sprinter' unit No 156419 about to depart from platform 4 with the 13.25 to Aberystwyth; this train originated as the 12.17 from Birmingham New Street. The major difference in the pictures is that platform 3, from which the pictures were taken, is now closed, both up and down trains now using platform 4. *Both RS*

The first view, taken on 23 April 1966, shows 4-6-0 No 75012 departing from platform 4 at Shrewsbury with the down 'Cambrian Coast Express'. At this point the line crosses the River Severn, and does not cross it again until just south of Arley.

In the present-day scene Class '156' unit No 156403, coupled to Class '150' unit No 150103 (see page 14), also departs from platform 4, with the 15.25 to Aberystwyth (14.17 ex-New Street). Unlike the previous two pictures, by walking a few yards down platform 3 one can soon see that obvious changes have occurred. Platform 3 has been shortened and some trackwork has been taken away. Also, in the 1966 picture the signals are lower quadrant with wooden posts, and these have been replaced with the upper quadrant type on metal poles, but still a pleasing sight. The splendid nameboard has disappeared, but the station's name is still there on top of the lighting pole to the left of the signals. On the right (looking unchanged!) is Shrewsbury prison. *Both RS*

These next two pictures at Shrewsbury show more than anything the changes that are occurring at the station. On 25 October 1966 Standard 4-6-0 No 75016 waits in bay platform No 1 with a parcels van prior to moving out to platform 4 to take out the down 'Cambrian Coast Express' (see page 11). At No 2 bay platform is a Swindon 'Cross Country' unit with an afternoon train to Llanelly via the Central Wales route. In the top left-hand corner of the picture can be seen Laura's Tower, part of Shrewsbury Castle. This picture also shows how well the design of the station architecture fits in with the castle.

The 'present' picture shows the same scene some 28 years later, on 2 August 1994. The bay platforms are no longer in use, the trackwork has been taken up, platforms 2 and 3 have been shortened, and the weeds are now growing through. *Both RS*

No view of Shrewsbury would be complete without a picture of the magnificent LNWR signal box situated at the southern end of the station at the junction of the lines to the south and west and the line to Wolverhampton. This is also a reminder that Shrewsbury was a joint station between the LMS and GWR. The first scene shows ex-LMS 'Black 5' 4-6-0 No 44856 coming off the Wolverhampton route on 25 October 1966 with a northbound freight and heading through the station on the line adjacent to platform 3. Severn Valley trains usually arrived and departed from platform 6, and these lines can be seen at the base of the signal box. Although by this time passenger services from Shrewsbury to Bridgnorth and Bewdley had finished, the line was still open to Berrington, some 4¼ miles south of Shrewsbury, for use in testing Rolls-Royce/Sentinel diesel locomotives; this section closed in January 1968.

In the second picture, taken on 6 August 1994, Class '150' unit No 150103 rounds the curve into platform 4 with the 14.17 from New Street, going forward to Aberystwyth. The splendid box is still there, now happily preserved, but the water tower has gone and the track has been rationalised; platform 3 has been shortened, giving a different perspective to the picture. *Both RS*

This next picture was taken from the end of platform 2 at Shrewsbury, and shows Standard Class '4MT' 4-6-0 No 75016 leaving with the down 'Cambrian Coast Express' on 25 October 1966 (see page 13). Everything in this picture denotes the approach to a busy station: there is an abundance of semaphore signals, lineside huts, water crane, and neat trackwork with a variety of points - all in all, a total railway scene.

Looking at the same scene some 28 years later, on 6 August 1994, we see Class '158' unit No 158816 heading south with the 13.33 Manchester Piccadilly to Cardiff service. The fine signal box is still there, but apart from a couple of semaphore signals the railway scene has changed almost out of all recognition. Platforms 1 and 2 are obviously no longer used, the trackwork has been lifted and platform 2 has been shortened considerably. The huts have also disappeared, and nature has taken over. However, despite all this change, Shrewsbury Abbey remains as a magnificent monument to a bygone age. But even this suffered from progress; when the railway was built, the Abbey's refectory had to be demolished to make way for the sidings, which were then overlooked by the only surviving part, the pulpit on the wall, from where the Bible used to be read aloud during mealtimes. *Both RS*

On 24 September 1960 ex-GWR Class '3MT' 0-6-0 No 3207 approaches Sutton Bridge Junction with a breakdown crane and support coach bound for the Welshpool area. In the background is Shrewsbury shed with a variety of locomotives to be seen, including 'Black 5' 4-6-0 No 45448 and Fowler Class '4MT' 2-6-4 tank No 42305. The Severn Valley lines can be seen on the right of the picture diverging in front of the locomotive.

In the picture of the same location taken on 6 August 1994, the shed area has vanished completely. However, some of the sidings to the left of the running lines remain, as also do the semaphore signals. The train is the 15.33 Manchester Piccadilly to Cardiff service, with '158' unit No 158863 in charge. *Michael Mensing/RS*

Class '5MT' 4-6-0 No 45285 is pictured on the turntable at Shrewsbury shed on 28 May 1966. As Shrewsbury was a joint line station there were originally two sheds on this site, GWR and LMS. It then came under the control of the Western Region, with the shed code 89A, but during the mid-1960s it reverted to the London Midland Region control.

Apart from the vast flat area, on 6 August 1994 there is nothing to indicate that a busy locomotive shed ever stood in this location. *Both RS*

Redundant ex-GWR 'Manor' Class 4-6-0 No 7812, formerly *Earlstoke Manor*, and behind it No 7820 *Dinmore Manor*, await their fate at Shrewsbury shed on 23 April 1966. For many years this famous class of locomotives had performed sterling work on the Cambrian Coast routes, and it is nice to know that both these locomotives avoided the breaker's torch and have been saved, No 7812 on the Severn Valley Railway by the Earlstoke Manor Fund.

It is hard to imagine, looking at the same area on 6 August 1994, that there was ever a shed here. *Both RS*

Back on the main line again, we see Class '4MT' 4-6-0 No 75006 approaching Sutton Bridge Junction signal box with the down 'Cambrian Coast Express' on Saturday 28 May 1966. The Severn Valley line can be seen swinging away behind the signal box, then in a few yards the Cambrian lines will leave the main line to Hereford and the south, and diverge away to the west. Shrewsbury shed can be seen in the background.

The same location on 6 August 1994 sees Class '158' unit No 158786 forming the 16.17 Birmingham New Street to Aberystwyth service. The locomotive shed disappeared many years ago, but the junction signal box is still with us. Also the trackbed of the Severn Valley line can still be seen clearly. The track layout has, however, altered: the junction for the Cambrian line is now just north of the box instead of south. There are also still some sidings to be seen, and semaphore signals, but no water crane, of course. Just before the signal box is a pedestrian bridge, which was installed some years ago, probably because the road bridge, on which the photographer stood to take both pictures, is now considered too dangerous for pedestrian traffic, being very narrow. *Both RS*

2
SHREWSBURY TO BUILDWAS

We are now on the Severn Valley line proper, just a few yards from Sutton Bridge Junction. The picture shows the rear view of ex-GWR railcar No 26, forming the 4.20 pm Shrewsbury to Kidderminster service on 24 September 1960. This railcar was one of a group built in 1940 and, along with others of the class, was part of the regular traction on the route. As can be seen, the line was double track for a short distance, although the bulk of the route was single.

In the picture of the same scene taken on the 6 August 1994, it would appear that the old trackbed now forms the road to serve a new housing estate, but otherwise it is difficult to imagine that a railway line had ever run through here. *Michael Mensing/RS*

The first station out of Shrewsbury on the Severn Valley route was Berrington, some 4 miles to the south-east of the Shropshire county town. On the afternoon of 4 June 1962 ex-GWR Class '4MT' 2-6-2 tank No 4147, with a brake-van, is seen heading north through the station with a return trip working from Buildwas Power Station.

It is now impossible to take a picture here from the road bridge north of the station because of the growth of trees, etc. Happily, however, the station house has been well preserved, and is now owned by Mr and Mrs Graham, who kindly gave the author permission to take this photograph on 6 August 1994. Although taken from ground level, the picture shows the station trackbed, with the southbound platform in good order, and some of the northbound platform intact. The canopy is still there over the booking hall and waiting room and, together with the station house, everything looks very attractive, a fine reminder of earlier times. *John Tennant/RS*

For the first few miles out of Shrewsbury the line roughly follows the River Severn, but around a mile or so to the west of it. At the village of Cound, some 7 miles from Shrewsbury, the line and river are much closer together and, apart from a couple of deviations, this remains the case until Stourport on Severn, some 38 miles from Shrewsbury. This shot, taken in 1962 looking towards the south-east, shows Cound Halt; this wooden structure was typical of the style found on the route. On the right-hand side is the rear of the Cound Lodge Hotel, with a right of way at the end of the platform to the river and a ferry, which then operated probably for the benefit of fishermen.

In the present-day photograph, taken on 10 September 1994, we can still see the trackbed of the railway, but most of the area has now become a beer garden and picnic area for the hotel, which incidentally still sells fishing permits. *Lens of Sutton/RS (courtesy of the proprietor of the Cound Lodge Hotel)*

As with Berrington, Cressage station house, some 4 miles further on, is now in private use. In the 'past' picture we see the station on 11 March 1961, playing host to the 9.50 am Shrewsbury to Bridgnorth train with No 4011O in charge. These ex-LMS Class '3MT' 2-6-2 tanks were designed by Stanier and introduced in 1935.

The 'present' picture, taken on 10 September 1994 (by kind permission of Mrs Foster) shows the station and area as it is today. Except for the windows, the station looks very similar, complete with canopy, but bushes and trees now grow where the trackbed was, and the platforms have disappeared. *John Dew/RS*

Buildwas, 12¼ miles from Shrewsbury, was possibly the most important junction station on the route, as well as being the railhead for the original Ironbridge Power Station, built in 1932, and having extensive sidings to serve it. Buildwas Junction was opened in 1862 along with the rest of the Severn Valley line from Shrewsbury to Hartlebury, and was a two-level junction station, the lower level being for the SVR and the upper for the Craven Arms-Wellington line (see the station plan opposite). In April 1957 an unidentified ex-LMS Fowler 2-6-4 tank pauses at Buildwas Junction with the 11.25 am Hartlebury-Shrewsbury service. On the right-hand side can clearly be seen the platform for the Wellington-Craven Arms branch, with a passenger train for Much Wenlock about to depart. On the left-hand side can be seen the original Ironbridge, or Buildwas, Power Station and the extensive sidings.

In today's photograph only the hills in the background tell us that this is the same location. A new Ironbridge 'B' Power Station, commissioned in 1970, was built on the western side of the junction station (right-hand side of the picture) and has fully mechanised facilities for handling 'Merry-go-round' (MGR) trains from Madeley Junction and beyond. Although the original Power Station was taken out of use in the 1970s, some of the buildings remain, but are obscured by trees in the 1994 picture. Most of the station area and sidings are now a golf course. *Geoff Bannister/RS*

Another 1950s view of Buildwas Junction, this time from the western side, showing the high-level platform and ex-GWR 0-6-0 pannier tank No 3732 leaving with the 11.35 am Much Wenlock-Wellington passenger train on 25 September 1954. *Geoff Bannister*

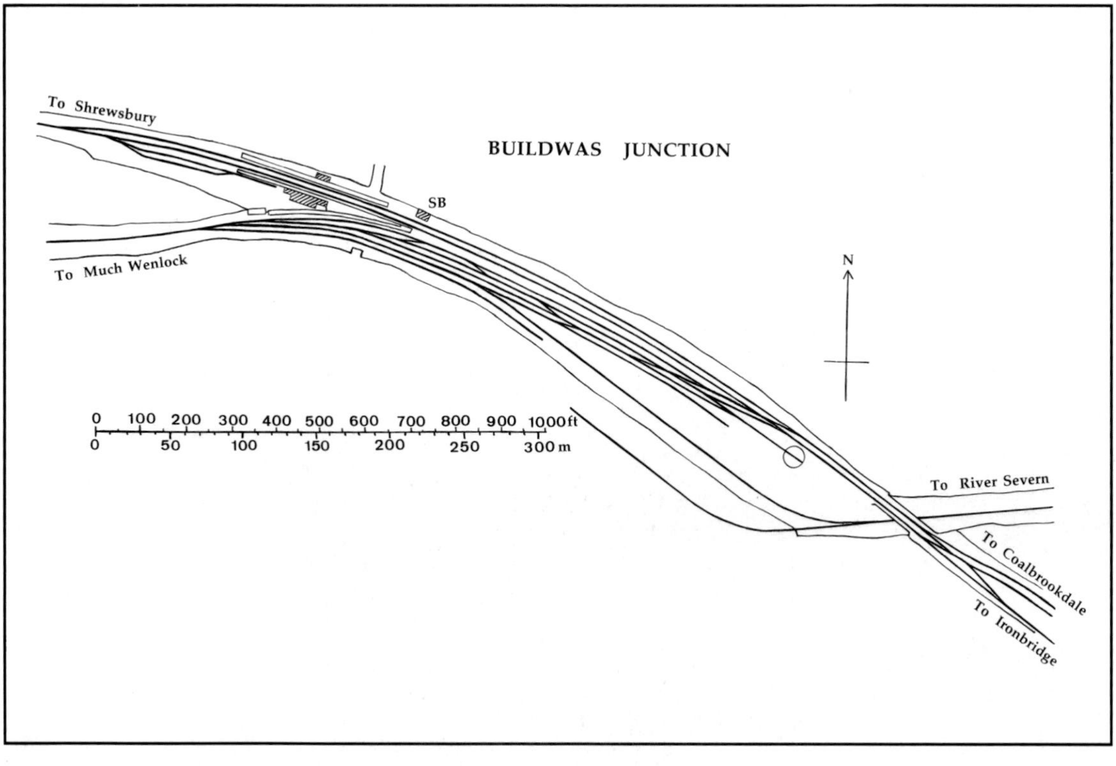

To the east of Buildwas on the line towards Wellington was Lightmoor Junction, which was the junction of the Wellington and Madeley lines, both of these places lying on the Wolverhampton-Shrewsbury route. The Wellington line completed a through route from Shrewsbury to Craven Arms in the west (via Much Wenlock), while that from Madeley Junction to Ironbridge Power Station (Buildwas) is the only surviving route in this complex of lines, which also included the LNWR Coalport-Oakengates line connecting Stafford with the industrial Ironbridge Gorge area. The 'past' picture, taken on 9 June 1962, shows 2-6-2 tank No 41201 crossing Coalbrookdale viaduct with the 5.40 pm Much Wenlock to Wellington train. This line, which opened in the 1860s, was closed to passengers in 1962.

The second picture shows the same location on 10 September 1994, with Class '56' No 56029 heading west for Ironbridge Power Station with an MGR train from Madeley Junction. In over 30 years not a great deal seems to have changed; we even have a Standard 8 or 10 of early 1960s vintage competing with today's cars. *Michael Mensing/RS*

To the west of Buildwas Junction was the line to Much Wenlock and Craven Arms, completing the link to Wellington. The section from Craven Arms to Much Wenlock was closed to passengers in 1951, but the passenger service from the latter to Wellington carried on until 1962. In a delightful scene at Much Wenlock on 5 May 1957 a youthful admirer watches the arrival of the 12.48 pm (Saturdays only) mixed train from Ketley (just over a mile south of Wellington), hauled by ex-GWR 0-6-0 pannier tank No 3732, one of a batch introduced in 1933 and designed by Collett for shunting and light goods work. Because there was only one platform at Much Wenlock, passenger trains could not be crossed here. There was, however, an extensive goods yard and shed, as well as a single-road locomotive shed, but the latter closed at the end of 1951 when the passenger service to Craven Arms was withdrawn.

This is the scene today, with the station having been converted into three houses and their gardens taking over the station area and trackbed. 10 September 1994. *Geoff Bannister/RS*

Our next stop on this 28-mile route is Longville, 10 miles from Craven Arms. On 25 September 1954 (three years after the closure of the line to passenger traffic) pannier tank No 3732 arrives at Longville station with the daily freight from Much Wenlock. From the previous pictures it will be seen that No 3732 was a regular performer on this line, being shedded at Wellington (84H).

On 10 September 1994 the station building and platform are still there, plus the nameboard, albeit in a different place. *Geoff Bannister/RS*

3
ON TO BRIDGNORTH

Back on the SVR line, here is a pleasant evening scene at Ironbridge & Broseley, as single unit No W55005 waits to leave with the 4.20 pm Shrewsbury to Hartlebury train on the penultimate day of the passenger service, 6 September 1963. From the opening of the line this was a crossing station.

The station area is now a car park, as can be seen in the present-day picture, taken on 10 September 1994. The only real point of identification is the houses that appear above and to the right of the station nameboard in the 1963 view and above the 'Disabled badge-holders' notice in 1994. *Hugh Ballantyne/RS*

On Monday 30 March 1959 Standard Class '3MT' 2-6-2 No 82008 pulls out of Ironbridge & Broseley station with the 1.45 pm Shrewsbury to Bewdley train. To the right of the locomotive can be seen the famous cast-iron bridge, built in 1777. This scene also shows the steepness of the gorge, making it a very attractive location. Just north of the station the line ran over a ten-arch brick and stone viaduct, built into the hillside.

As in the previous modern view, with the exception of the wall in the bottom left-hand corner, the whole station area has now become a car park. Happily the iron bridge, the first in the world, is still with us, although the steepness of the gorge nearly destroyed it by slipping and squeezing the footings together. These have been braced by setting a great concrete bar underwater, holding them apart. The bridge is closed to vehicular traffic, but remains a proud monument to a bygone industrial age. Indeed, the whole area around Ironbridge is now one vast industrial museum, attracting visitors from worldwide to the birthplace of the Industrial Revolution. *Michael Mensing/RS*

A mile after leaving Ironbridge we come to the small settlement of Jackfield, which was once famous for Maws tile factory, and a mirror-like shiny black glaze. This factory closed many years ago, but has now been reopened as a museum, being part of the Ironbridge Gorge Museum, thus adding to the uniqueness of the area. The line ran right by the Maws factory, with sidings for the same, and also a small halt. In the first view, taken on 15 October 1960, we see the rear of an unidentified ex-GWR railcar, setting off with the 4.20 pm Shrewsbury to Kidderminster service. The Maws factory can be seen on the left-hand side. *John Dew*

The second photograph, taken in 1962, shows a closer view of the halt, almost a 'carbon copy' of Cound Halt. *Lens of Sutton*

In the present-day view, taken on 16 September 1994, the trackbed of the line is now a walkway, but just above the gate can be seen the parapet of the road underbridge, which can also be seen in the middle picture.

Jackfield had in fact two halts; the original was opened in 1934, but had to be replaced because of the danger of landslip. The halt featured in these pictures, a quarter of a mile nearer Bridgnorth, was opened in 1954. *RS*

Half a mile from Jackfield Halt was Coalport (GWR) station. On the eastern side of the river was Coalport's other station, the terminus of the former LNWR line from Oakengates, and Wellington for Stafford. Coalport is also world-famous for its chinaware, especially floral designs. In June 1962 an unidentified Standard Class '3MT' 2-6-2 tank pulls out of the GWR station with a Shrewsbury train. Note the station garden.

The 'present' picture, take on 16 September 1994, shows the splendid station house, now in private use. Both platforms and the trackbed are still there, as is the small waiting room on the northbound side, obscured by the trees. *John Tennant/RS*

After leaving Coalport the line leaves the Severn Gorge and the industrial area. The next station is Linley Halt, just over 18 miles from Shrewsbury. This was the most isolated station on the route; built to serve the nearby Apley estate, it had no public road access. Apley Hall, on the eastern side of the line, was connected to the station by a suspension bridge over the River Severn, the bridge replacing a ferry. In the first picture we see Linley Halt in 1962, looking towards Shrewsbury. On the left-hand side of the station was a goods siding, but this was closed in 1951, and what was Linley Station became Linley Halt.

Today's view shows the fine station house now in private hands, and the platform and trackbed, now used by a different form of motive power! *Lens of Sutton/RS*

Between Linley and Bridgnorth, just over 4 miles in distance, the line followed the Severn through some very pleasant and fertile meadowland and, as this picture shows, ran along the eastern edge of Bridgnorth Golf Course, situated a mile north of the town. This scene, taken on 30 August 1962, shows a northbound coal train headed by ex-GWR Class '4MT' 2-6-2 tank No 4129.

The same scene was photographed on 16 September 1994 and shows the new clubhouse; beyond the trees where the trackbed was, the golf course has been extended, and now occupies both sides of the line. The contours of the distant hills confirm the location. *Michael Mensing/RS*

4
BRIDGNORTH

Bridgnorth station, which was opened in 1862, as were all the principal stations on the route, is approached from the town by a long driveway. There was also access to Castle Hill and Bridgnorth High Town by a footbridge across the valley, but this was closed in 1976. However, a new footbridge was completed and opened in 1994, thanks to the efforts of the Bridgnorth Footbridge Trust. In July 1962 Class '2MT' 2-6-2 tank No 41202 enters Bridgnorth station with a southbound afternoon passenger train from Shrewsbury. At the rear of the train, just out of sight, is the 550-yard-long tunnel that passed beneath Bridgnorth High Town. The tunnel was built on a double curve swinging to the right, then to the left.

Today's picture shows some changes compared to that of over 30 years ago. The signal box is not the original, this replacement building coming from Pensnett on the Wolverhampton-Wombourne-Stourbridge line. The original goods shed is still there, sandwiched between the new shed and the large repair depot. New houses can now be seen around the approach to the tunnel. The train in this 23 August 1994 picture is the rear of the 1.20 pm to Kidderminster, hauled by ex-WD 2-10-0 locomotive No 600 *Gordon*. In BR days both northbound and southbound trains used both platforms, and today's SVR trains also arrive at and depart from both.
John Tennant/RS

In the summer of 1965, when Mr Keith Beddoes of Kidderminster and a group of fellow railway enthusiasts came up with the idea of preserving the SVR southwards from Bridgnorth, it nearly ended in disaster, because on 25 July 1965 dismantling was resumed at Bridgnorth. But the enthusiasts, now known as the Severn Valley Railway Society, managed to persuade BR to stop the demolition work - and the rest is history.

In BR days Bridgnorth never possessed a locomotive shed, and originally the SVR used the old goods shed and sidings for the shed area. This scene, taken over 20 years ago on 7 July 1974, shows the locomotive yard as it was then. On shed are ex-LMS '4MT' 2-6-0 No 43106 being coaled and Class '2MT' 2-6-0 No 46521. Beyond these locomotives are 'Black 5' 4-6-0 No 45110 and '8F' 2-8-0 No 8233 (now 48773). On the left-hand side of the picture are locomotives and boilers at various stages of repair.

What a contrast is today's scene, taken on 28 August 1994, showing the excellent three-road shed and surrounding area and facilities. This shed, which is also a workshop, came into use in May 1978. Visible on shed are Standard Class '4MT' 2-6-4 tank No 80079, ex-GWR '43xx' Class 2-6-0 No 7325, ex-GWR '57xx' 0-6-0 pannier tank No 5764, and 'Western' Class diesel-hydraulic No D1062 *Western Courier*. *Both RS*

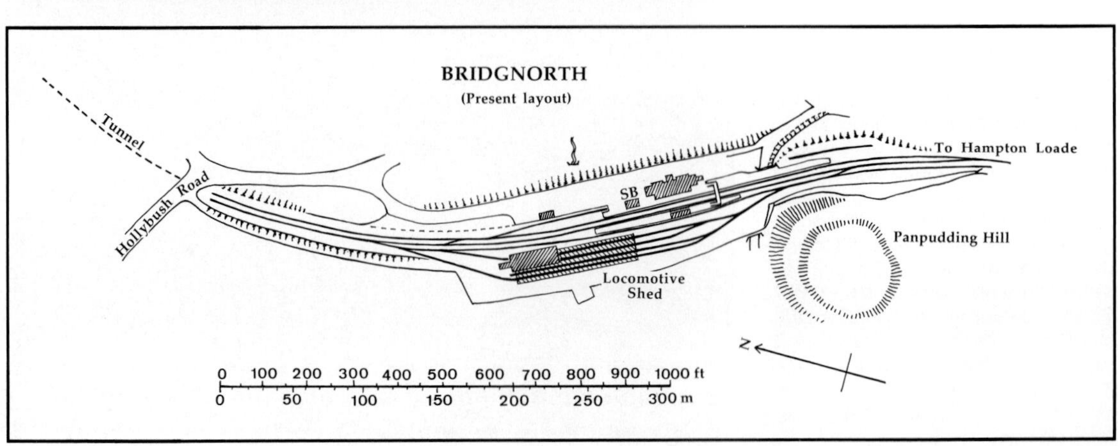

On the penultimate day of the passenger service, 6 September 1963, 2-6-2 tank No 41207 stands at a rather forlorn-looking Bridgnorth station with the 1.45 pm Shrewsbury to Kidderminster train. On the left-hand side of the picture can be seen the goods sidings and a mixture of sheds looking as if they have seen more prosperous days.

The same scene seven years later, on 27 December 1970, shows ex-GWR diesel railcar No 22 reversing into platform 2 at Bridgnorth. This railcar was often used in the early days of the SVR, especially on 'shoppers' specials' from Hampton Loade to Bridgnorth. It is now to be found at the GWR Society's depot at Didcot. On the left-hand side of the picture is ex-GWR Class '3MT' 0-6-0 No 3205, also a frequent performer in the early days of the preserved line, and which hauled the first regular passenger service out of Bridgnorth to Hampton Loade on Saturday 23 May 1970. Although members' trains for Hampton Loade had been run since 1968, the Light Railway Order was only granted to the SVR in May 1970.

In the third view, taken on 28 August 1994, 2-10-0 No 600 *Gordon* prepares to leave Bridgnorth with the 1.20 pm to Kidderminster - the return working of the 'Severn Valley Limited', which conveys restaurant cars each Sunday from 13 March until 30 October. The new shed area can be seen on the left, and platform 1 (right-hand side) has been lengthened considerably to accommodate longer trains. The trackwork has also been modified. *Hugh Ballantyne/RS (2)*

Early days on the preserved SVR, as 2-6-0 No 46443 waits to leave Bridgnorth with a members-only trip to Hampton Loade on 1 September 1968. On the right-hand side is outside-cylinder ex-industrial locomotive No 4 (built by Peckett in 1928, works number 1738, for Hams Hall Power Station at Coleshill, near Birmingham) giving brake-van rides. There is also a very mixed selection of rolling-stock in the distant siding.

We can now view the same scene some 26 years later, on 15 August 1994, as '8F' No 48773 runs round the stock of the 4.00 pm to Kidderminster service. The trackwork has been slightly modified, and a splendid GWR bracket signal has been installed. Fencing now protects the pathway on the right-hand side, platform 1 has been lengthened considerably, the hut has disappeared, and the stock in the siding looks very different! And of course today people are not allowed to wander round the site as they were in the very early days of preservation - a lineside pass is now needed. *Both RS*

Soon after leaving Bridgnorth station the line crosses the B4363 Cleobury Mortimer road. On 1 April 1974 'J94' Class 0-6-0 saddle tank No 193 passes over the road and heads for Hampton Loade with the 1.00 pm train from Bridgnorth.

The same view 20 years later, on 15 August 1994,sees ex-GWR 2-8-0 No 2857 running light into Bridgnorth station in order to take out the 5.15 pm to Kidderminster. The road has been straightened out and marked, and new lighting has been installed. The road level has also been slightly raised; according to the new sign, the gap is now 13 feet clearance between the road and the bridge, and not 13 ft 9 in as in the earlier picture. The driveway in the bottom right-hand corner of the picture now leads to a new house, and not to a field as in the previous view. *Both RS*

When the Light Railway Order for the SVR line was first applied for, at the beginning of 1968, Shropshire County Council objected because of the cost of building a railway bridge (estimated at £50,000 to £60,000) over the proposed Bridgnorth bypass. A public enquiry was held into this, and in June 1969 it was decided that the objections should be dismissed and the application granted. However, the Minister of Transport overruled the decision and refused the application, but left the way open for the SVR Company to negotiate with Shropshire County Council. In 1969 the SVR Company decided that it would, at its own expense, provide a bridge over the bypass, and with this the County Council withdrew its main objection to the Light Railway Order.

It was to be over 15 years before the bypass was completed, opening on 29 March 1985. In the intervening years, because of the problem of the cost of the bypass bridge, proposals were put forward to abandon the station site at Bridgnorth, but these proposals were voted down and it was decided to raise the money for the new bridge. It would be hard to imagine today the SVR without its Bridgnorth station!

At the end of the day, through negotiation with the County Council and the Government, it was agreed that the SVR would pay 30 per cent of the cost of the bridge and the County Council the rest, the total cost being around £105,000. So for just over £30,000, considerably less than the original estimate of the total cost approaching £60,000, the future of the SVR was secured.

In the first picture, taken on 21 November 1981, in pre-bypass days, ex-LMS 'Jubilee' Class 4-6-0 Mo 5690 *Leander* heads out of Bridgnorth with a special train for Hampton Loade.

The same location today shows the edge of the bypass and the new bridge. The train is the 5.15 pm to Kidderminster, hauled by 2-8-0 No 2857, and the date is 15 August 1994. *Both RS*

5
SOUTH TOWARDS BEWDLEY

For the first mile and a half out of Bridgnorth, southbound trains face a stiff climb for the most part at around 1 in 100. On 26 May 1973 'Black 5' 4-6-0 No 45110 climbs the gradient over Oldbury viaduct with the 3.00 pm Bridgnorth-Hampton Loade train. This five-arch viaduct, originally built for double track for a previous scheme, crosses above Daniel's Mill, complete with water wheel.

The same scene, taken on 3 October 1994 but from a higher vantage point because the trees framing the viaduct in the previous picture have been removed, allowing the signal to be incorporated into the picture. The viaduct was considerably rebuilt in 1975/76. The train is an engineers' special, hauled by English Electric Class '50' locomotive No 50044 *Exeter*. *Both RS*

A few hundred yards south from Oldbury viaduct is the short tunnel at Knowlesands, also of double-track width. On 13 October 1974 ex-GWR pannier tank No 5764 heads out of the tunnel with an afternoon Bewdley-Bridgnorth train. The summit of the south-bound climb out of Bridgnorth is approximately a quarter of a mile south of the tunnel, but the tunnel area is on the level.

Twenty years later, on 8 October 1994, '8F' 2-8-0 No 48773 leaves Knowlesands tunnel with the 10.25 am Kidderminster-Bridgnorth service. *Both RS*

After the summit of the climb out of Bridgnorth, southbound trains then descend Eardington bank. This picture, taken on 30 August 1962, shows Standard Class '3MT' 2-6-2 tank No 82001 heading down the 1 in 100 with the 1.45 pm Shrewsbury-Kidderminster train. The location is a quarter of a mile north of Eardington Halt.

Today's picture, taken on 15 August 1994, shows Class '2MT' 2-6-0 No 46521 in charge of the 2.45 pm Bridgnorth-Kidderminster train. The principal change between the two pictures is that the bushes and trees have grown. *Michael Mensing/RS*

Left and right In 1972, when this picture was taken, Eardington Halt was much used by the SVR as an intermediate stopping place with watering facilities. On 3 August of that year No 46443 prepares to leave the halt with an afternoon Hampton Loade-Bridgnorth train. Work is in hand to reinstate the siding; note the loading-gauge over the trackbed towards the rear of the train.

Below and below right The first picture of Eardington Halt was taken in 1962 and clearly shows the siding and loading-gauge as well as the station buildings.

Today's view, taken on 18 September 1994, shows that the ground next to the siding has been

On 15 August 1994 No 46521, also a Class '2MT' 2-6-0, climbs the 1 in 200 through the now closed station with the 1.00 pm Kidderminster-Bridgnorth service. Eardington Halt was closed in 1982, and the siding that was reinstated is used for storing breakdown and PW equipment. *Both RS*

banked up and a breakdown train now occupies the siding. Note also the water tank and column, an addition since BR days. The train approaching is the 12 noon service from Kidderminster to Bridgnorth, with No 46443 in charge, complete with a 'Thomas The Tank Engine' face. The annual 'Thomas' weekend is very popular with youngsters who pack the trains, along with mums and dads, to capacity. *Lens of Sutton/RS*

A mile north of Eardington Halt, the River Severn swings almost a mile to the east of the line for a short distance, but below Eardington, where the Bridgnorth-Highley road runs under the track at Hay Bridge, it is within a few yards of the line. In the recent past landslips have occurred in this area, so speed restrictions are usually in operation. Within a mile or so Hampton Loade is reached, which in the first few years of the SVR was the southern terminus of the passenger operation. The service to Bewdley did not commence until 1974, and that to Kidderminster until 1984. On a very cold 31 December 1973 0-6-0 saddle tank No 193 prepares to leave Hampton Loade with the 3.30 pm train to Bridgnorth. The station originally had only one platform on the west side, but another platform was added in 1883.

Today's view, taken 20 years later on 28 August 1994, shows only superficial changes. Benches, trollies and milk churns now adorn the platforms, 'new vintage' lighting has been installed, and there are vans in the sidings. Hampton Loade still boasts a ferry across the River Severn. *Both RS*

A view of the other end of Hampton Loade station on 15 April 1968, a few months before the end of steam on British Railways, as 2-6-0 No 46443 runs round its train before taking a members-only special back to Bridgnorth. *RS*

This delightful view taken around 1920 at Hampton Loade shows presumably the Station Master and his son at the lower end of the northbound platform. The similar view taken over 70 years later, on 28 August 1994, shows how well the SVR manages to recreate the past. *John Tennant collection/RS*

Just over a mile south of Hampton Loade were Alveley colliery sidings, built to serve Alveley colliery, situated on the other side of the river. The colliery was connected to the sidings by means of an aerial ropeway over a concrete bridge, and this view, taken on 21 October 1961 shows the ropeway in action. The picture was taken from the railway side of the river.

The colliery was closed early in 1969 and the sidings dismantled. The present-day scene, on 18 September 1994, shows the fine-looking bridge still in place, but instead of leading to a colliery it now leads walkers to a country park. *John Dew/RS*

A few hundred yards past the colliery sidings was situated Alveley Halt, provided specifically for the colliery workers and not mentioned in the timetables. This view of the halt, looking towards Bridgnorth, was also taken on 21 October 1961.

The same location on 18 September 1994 shows that the halt has disappeared, but the crossing is still there. This leads to the golf course that lies between the SVR and the river, although the golf clubhouse itself is on the other side of the line. *John Dew/RS*

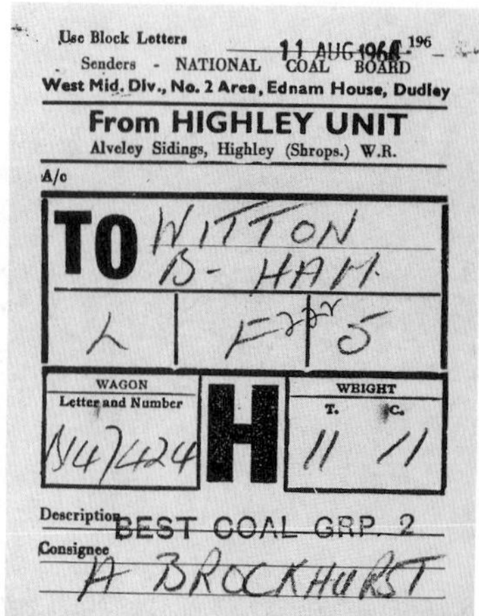

Use Block Letters 11 AUG 1964 196

Senders - NATIONAL COAL BOARD

West Mid. Div., No. 2 Area, Ednam House, Dudley

From HIGHLEY UNIT

Alveley Sidings, Highley (Shrops.) W.R.

A/c

TO WITTON B-HAM

WAGON Letter and Number N47424

H

WEIGHT T. C. 11 11

Description BEST COAL GRP. 2

Consignee A BROCKHURST

Around half a mile from the site of Alveley Halt is Highley station, winner of major awards (together with Arley) in the Best Restored Station competition, as well as featuring in many film and TV productions. Even in the past, the station was always very smart, as can be seen in the first view, taken in the late 1950s. On the right-hand side can be seen the edge of the footbridge, which, due to deterioration after the closure of the station in 1963, finally had to be demolished by the SVR in 1974.

Highley station in all its glory is seen on 22 August 1994. Looking at this scene, it is easy to see how it comes to win awards; everything is really immaculate. *Author's collection/RS*

On 7 October 1959 ex-GWR 0-6-0 pannier tank No 2118 pulls round the curve into Highley station's lone platform with a southbound passenger train. Dominating the scene is the fine stone-built Station Master's house. This picture was obviously taken from the station footbridge glimpsed in the previous photograph.

After the station was closed in 1963 very little demolition work took place, but much work was still needed to restore the station and area to today's condition. The first passenger trains from Bridgnorth to Highley started running in April 1974 and in the second picture, taken on a wet 13 August of that year, one of the mainstays of the SVR's locomotive fleet in the early days, ex-LMS '4MT' 2-6-0 No 43106, runs into Highley with a Bridgnorth-Bewdley train. The service to Bewdley had commenced in May 1974, after a bridge just beyond Highley had been rebuilt. This view shows the signal box (which remained intact from BR days) and also one of the bases of the then recently demolished footbridge.

Twenty years further on, on 22 August 1994, '8F' No 48773 pulls into the station with the 11.00 am from Bridgnorth going forward to Kidderminster. The token exchange is now done from the lineside and not from the platform, as in the earlier view. Subtle but distinctive changes have taken place to the station. The TV aerials have disappeared, and so has the chimney and modern-looking roof on the gents' toilet. The hanging baskets are now much larger and more magnificent, there are now flowers at the front of the Station Master's house, and the base of the old footbridge has now become a flower bed. Note also the elegant lamp-posts, the finishing touch. *R. J. Sellick/RS (2)*

As well as Alveley colliery to the north of Highley, there was also Highley colliery just to the west of the station, roughly a third of the way on the mile-long journey from the station to the town. However, shortly after Alveley colliery opened in 1939, Highley colliery was closed for winding coal. As well as mining, Highley was also (and still is) a farming area, and this next picture, taken on 13 August 1974, shows on the right-hand side the remains of the cattle dock. The train is an afternoon Bewdley-Bridgnorth service, hauled by 2-6-0 No 46443.

Today's picture, taken on 22 August 1994, shows not only the edge of the newly restored cattle dock, but also a 'parachute'-type water tank. This is extremely convenient because Highley is roughly the halfway point between Kidderminster and Bridgnorth. To complete the picture once again is 2-8-0 No 48773, in charge of the 1.00 pm Kidderminster to Bridgnorth train. Highley is well worth a visit, not only for the country parks adjacent to the station, but also for the historic mining village itself, complete with 12th-century Norman church, all set in beautiful south Shropshire. *Both RS*

After Highley our next port of call is Arley, a distance of just over 2 miles. The line runs through pleasant meadowlands, skirting the northern edge of the Wyre Forest as it approaches Arley station. This originally had only one platform, but like Hampton Loade another was added at a later date. The first picture shows the station on 25 May 1963 as smart-looking Class '3MT' 2-6-2 tank No 82005 enters the station with the 1.45 pm Shrewsbury to Kidderminster train.

After the station's closure in 1963 by BR, the up line and the signals were removed. Later on, thinking that it would no longer be needed, the SVR removed the signal box. The second picture shows the scene of dereliction just as restoration was beginning in April 1972.

The work was finally completed and the station re-opened in May 1974, in time for the new passenger service between Bridgnorth and Bewdley. The third view shows Arley station today, a credit to all the volunteers who helped to restore it. The train is the 12.15 pm Bridgnorth-Kidderminster hauled by No 48773, and the date is 15 August 1994. As with all the SVR stations, certain things have been added, such as trolleys and barrows, as well as vintage lighting, all adding to the ambience of the line. The new signal box is of LNWR style, and came from Yorton on the Shrewsbury-Crewe line. On the opposite river bank is the attractive village of Upper Arley, nowadays reached by a footbridge built to replace a ferry. *Brian Moone (2)/RS*

Here is a pleasant reminder that the SVR route (as did most of BR in those days) saw a fair amount of freight working. On 4 June 1960 ex-GWR Class '43xx' 2-6-0 No 6382 enters Arley station with the daily 10.25 am Hartlebury-Shrewsbury pick-up goods. The fireman is exchanging tokens with the Station Master/Signalman, the token machine being kept in the booking office.

The scene is repeated on 14 August 1994, only this time with a passenger train - 2-8-0 No 48773 is in charge of the 12.45 pm Kidderminster-Bridgnorth train. The token will be exchanged at the other end of the platform, opposite the signal box. It is worth noting that from time to time on special weekends, freight trains are run, and on occasions there are also specially chartered freights, run usually for photographic purposes for enthusiasts. *Brian Moone/RS*

So far on this journey we have travelled through the county of Shropshire, but a few yards from Arley station we enter the county of Worcestershire, and stay in that county for the remainder of our journey. As well as changing counties, the line crosses the River Severn just below Arley, by means of the famous Victoria Bridge, the first crossing since leaving Shrewsbury. This single-span cast-iron bridge was completed in 1861, and is similar to the Albert Edward Bridge at Buildwas, on the line to Wellington and Madeley Junction. On 27 May 1974, during the first few days of operating the passenger service to Bewdley, 2-6-0 No 43106 crosses the Victoria Bridge with an afternoon Bridgnorth-Bewdley train. This picture was taken from the eastern side of the line.

Two decades later, on 14 August 1994, 2-8-0 No 48773 crosses the famous bridge with the 11.05 am from Bridgnorth to Kidderminster. The scaffolding is in place for renovation work. *Both RS*

The late evening sun highlights the Victoria Bridge on the western side as the handsome ex-GWR '28xx' 2-8-0 No 2857 crosses with a Bridgnorth-Bewdley train on 20 September 1986. Note the beautifully restored LNER coaches, one of four sets of stock from four different railways, the others being GWR, LMS and SR. Between November 1979 and the end of February 1980 extensive repairs were carried out to the bridge, including new joists, replacement rivets, etc. The trackwork was also lifted and relaid, and the whole bridge was repainted. It was re-opened on 1 March 1980. *RS*

After crossing the river the line runs through a wooded area, then passes by Trimpley reservoirs and pumping station, and also an aqueduct, before Northwood Halt is reached. Pictured here (looking north) in 1962, the halt was opened in 1935, mainly for holidaymakers and anglers. It was closed in 1963, but re-opened in 1974 with the resumption of services to Bewdley.

As can be seen from the 13 September 1994 picture, it is today very much restored, complete with a far smarter waiting room. It is a request stop for trains, and is not included in the SVR timetable. The level crossing at the southern end of the halt (replacing the earlier hand-operated gates of BR days) is now protected by light signals and an audible warning. *Lens of Sutton/RS*

A picture that well illustrates the state of the line in the heavily wooded section between the Victoria Bridge and Bewdley at the end of the passenger service, and prior to the take-over by the SVR. The date is 30 June 1966, and '8F' No 48531, propelling a brake-van, heads north for Highley for another load of coal from Alveley colliery for the West Midlands power stations. The location is just south of Northwood Halt.

Twenty-eight years later, at the same spot, we see 'Western' Class diesel-hydraulic No D1062 *Western Courier* heading south with the 4.20 pm Bridgnorth to Kidderminster service on 14 August 1994. The trackwork on this section has been raised and relaid and the telegraph poles have disappeared, although in the bottom left-hand corner of the picture the anchorage of the stay wires for one of the poles can still be seen. *Both RS*

6
TENBURY WELLS LINE

Less than a mile south of Northwood Halt is the point where the line from Woofferton converged with the SVR, both lines running parallel with each other for around a mile to just before Bewdley station. The Woofferton line was closed in 1965, and in this 30 June 1966 picture of a Highley-Kidderminster coal train hauled by '8F' 2-8-0 No 48531, the disused trackbed can be seen clearly, swinging away to the left in the middle foreground; it then crosses the River Severn by means of a lattice bridge.

The same scene today clearly again shows the trackbed of the Woofferton line, but bushes and trees have taken over where the line swings away to the west. The train is the 1.20 pm Bridgnorth-Kidderminster, hauled by 2-10-0 No 600 *Gordon*. *Gordon* was built for the War Department in 1943 by the North British Locomotive Company of Glasgow, and spent all its life at the Longmoor Military Railway in Hampshire, being mainly used for instructional purposes. *Both RS*

At this appropriate point in the journey, we leave the SVR and take a glimpse at the line to Tenbury Wells and Woofferton, and also at the famous Cleobury Mortimer to Ditton Priors branch. The former was a joint line for the 5½ miles from Tenbury to Woofferton, owned by both the GWR and the LNWR companies. Our first picture, taken at Easton Court station, named after the local country house that was situated some distance from the station, shows GWR 0-4-2 tank No 1455 with the mid-afternoon Tenbury-Woofferton auto-train, pausing at the station on 24 August 1956. This station was always listed in the timetable as 'Station for Little Hereford', which was a quarter of a mile away, much nearer than the country house after which the station was named. A fine station house was situated on the single platform adjacent to the A456 Kidderminster-Woofferton road. At the western end of the station (left-hand side of the picture) there was a short siding that ran into a bay at the end of the platform; this was used for loading sugar beet, being a common crop in this fertile and well-watered area.

The Woofferton-Tenbury Wells section was closed in 1961, Tenbury to Cleobury Mortimer in 1964 and Cleobury to Bewdley in 1965. Fortunately, as can be seen from the 'present' photograph, Easton Court station is still very much intact and is now owned by Mr and Mrs Rhodes, who very kindly gave permission for this photograph to be taken on 2 September 1994. Apart from the station house, some of the platform is still there and the trackbed now forms the back garden. *Geoff Bannister/RS*

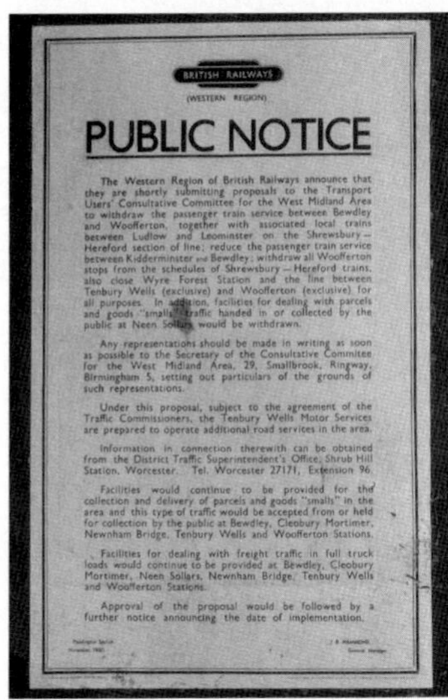

BRITISH RAILWAYS

(WESTERN REGION)

PUBLIC NOTICE

The Western Region of British Railways announce that they are shortly submitting proposals to the Transport Users' Consultative Committee for the West Midland Area to withdraw the passenger train service between Bewdley and Woofferton, together with associated local trains between Ludlow and Leominster on the Shrewsbury–Hereford section of line; reduce the passenger train service between Kidderminster and Bewdley; withdraw all Woofferton stops from the schedules of Shrewsbury–Hereford trains, also close Wyre Forest Station and the line between Tenbury Wells (exclusive) and Woofferton (exclusive) for all purposes. In addition, facilities for dealing with parcels and goods "smalls" traffic handed in or collected by the public at Neen Sollars would be withdrawn.

Any representations should be made in writing as soon as possible to the Secretary of the Consultative Commitee for the West Midland Area, 29, Smallbrook, Ringway, Birmingham 5, setting out particulars of the grounds of such representations.

Under this proposal, subject to the agreement of the Traffic Commissioners, the Tenbury Wells Motor Services are prepared to operate additional road services in the area.

Information in connection therewith can be obtained from the District Traffic Superintendent's Office, Shrub Hill Station, Worcester. Tel. Worcester 27171, Extension 96.

Facilities would continue to be provided for the collection and delivery of parcels and goods "smalls" in the area and this type of traffic would be accepted from or held for collection by the public at Bewdley, Cleobury Mortimer, Newnham Bridge, Tenbury Wells and Woofferton Stations.

Facilities for dealing with freight traffic in full truck loads would continue to be provided at Bewdley, Cleobury Mortimer, Neen Sollars, Newnham Bridge, Tenbury Wells and Woofferton Stations.

Approval of the proposal would be followed by a further notice announcing the date of implementation.

The November 1960 notice announcing the withdrawal of the passenger service and the closure of the line between Woofferton and Tenbury Wells, the closure of Wyre Forest station, and the reduction of the service between Kidderminster and Bewdley. *John Tennant*

Our next destination on this attractive country line, which ran through Worcestershire, Shropshire and Herefordshire, is Tenbury Wells. Ex-GWR diesel railcar No 22 (now preserved at Didcot and for a time to be seen on the SVR in the late 1960s and early 1970s) leaves Tenbury station with the 4.58 pm to Hartlebury on 15 August 1959, passing the distinctive signal box. Tenbury Wells station (or just plain Tenbury as it was known in the GWR timetables) was opened in 1861 and was situated some half a mile from this most pleasant of towns.

The site and surrounding area of Tenbury station is now owned by the Wells soft drink company, who kindly gave permission to obtain the 'present' picture. Looking at this factory scene, it is hard to imagine that there was ever a railway station here, except that part of the platform still remains on the left-hand side as a reminder of earlier days. *Michael Mensing/RS*

Cleobury Mortimer, just over 6 miles from Bewdley, was the junction for the famous Cleobury Mortimer & Ditton Priors Light Railway (CM&DPR). This line, which was opened in 1908, was closed to passenger traffic in 1938, but remained open for goods traffic. Then in 1957 the line was taken over from BR Western Region by the Admiralty, but was completely closed in 1965. On 18 September 1952 ex-CM&DPR ex-GWR 0-6-0 pannier tank No 29 (with outside cylinders), which was shedded at Kidderminster (85D), pulls through Burwarton station with a train from the Royal Navy Armament Depot, constructed in the last war at Ditton Priors, and heads for Cleobury Mortimer. Ditton Priors, the terminus of the line, is 11 miles north-west of Cleobury Mortimer. The wooden station waiting room and porters' room was of standard CM&DPR design, although the platform was raised by the GWR. Just south of the station there was an open road crossing, so there was a mandatory 10 mph speed limit on the crossing and its approaches.

The scene today, over 40 years later, on the evening of 2 September 1994 shows that part of the platform is still intact and the trackbed can still be made out. *Geoff Bannister/RS*

Back on the SVR again, at the convergence of the two routes on 20 June 1959, we see ex-GWR diesel railcar No 20 with the 3.05 pm Tenbury Wells-Kidderminster service. As was mentioned on page 58, these two routes ran parallel with each other until Bewdley station, where, just north of the station, there were crossover points giving trains from Kidderminster access to the Tenbury line and vice versa.

On 7 August 1994 ex-GWR 0-6-0 pannier tank No 5764 passes the same spot with the 3.35 pm from Bridgnorth to Kidderminster. The trackbed of the Woofferton line can be seen diverging to the left. *Michael Mensing/RS*

7
BEWDLEY

Bewdley, or Wribbenhall, viaduct, just to the north of Bewdley station, has seven arches and is 112 yards long. On 29 June 1966 '8F' 2-8-0 No 48531 propels a brake-van over the viaduct and heads north for Highley and the colliery sidings. By this time the Tenbury line had been removed, and in a few hundred yards the double track became single, as it remains right until the present day. At the near end of the viaduct is Bewdley North signal box, then obscured by trees.

In the 'present' picture, taken on 29 July 1994 and showing 2-6-0 No 46521 heading north for Bridgnorth with the 3.30 pm from Kidderminster, Bewdley North box can be seen clearly. The road in the foreground now has double yellow lines, and new houses have been built at the foot of the viaduct. With road widening, the attractive little garden in the left foreground seems to have partially disappeared. *Both RS*

These next four views show the northern approach to Bewdley station from the 1950s to the present day. The first scene, dating from 15 August 1959, shows ex-GWR diesel railcar No W22 arriving at the station with an afternoon train from Bridgnorth, going forward to Kidderminster. The BR three-car DMU in the background has worked into Bewdley as the 2.00 pm service from Birmingham Snow Hill and has moved out of the platform to make way for the railcar.

The second picture shows once again '8F' No 48531 approaching the station and heading for Stourport Power Station with a load of coal from Alveley colliery on 29 June 1966. The station lamps have changed and the GWR station benches have disappeared, but Bewdley North box is still there, as are the wooden signals and bracket signals. Although by this time the Tenbury line had closed, the crossover points were still in place (beneath the back of the locomotive tender) for access to the line from the Kidderminster direction.

On 18 May 1974 trains began running from Bridgnorth to Bewdley, and on the 26th (only the second weekend of the service) we see SVR stalwart ex-WD 2-10-0 *Gordon* entering Bewdley with an afternoon train from Bridgnorth. All these pictures were taken from the station footbridge, but by this time the trees had grown, obscuring the signal box. The crossover points have now gone and the bracket signal, although still there, is out of use. On the right-hand side new houses have been built.

The fourth picture in this quartet shows the SVR today, on 29 July 1994, as ex-GWR 'Mogul' No 7325 enters the station and makes for platform 3 with the 2.45 pm Bridgnorth-Kidderminster service; nowadays both northbound and southbound trains use all three platforms. The trees have been cut back once again, leaving a view of Bewdley North signal box and the wooden signals, but the other bracket signal has been removed. Benches have now returned to the station platforms, and the new lighting has been replaced by the type seen in the first picture. *Michael Mensing/ RS (3)*

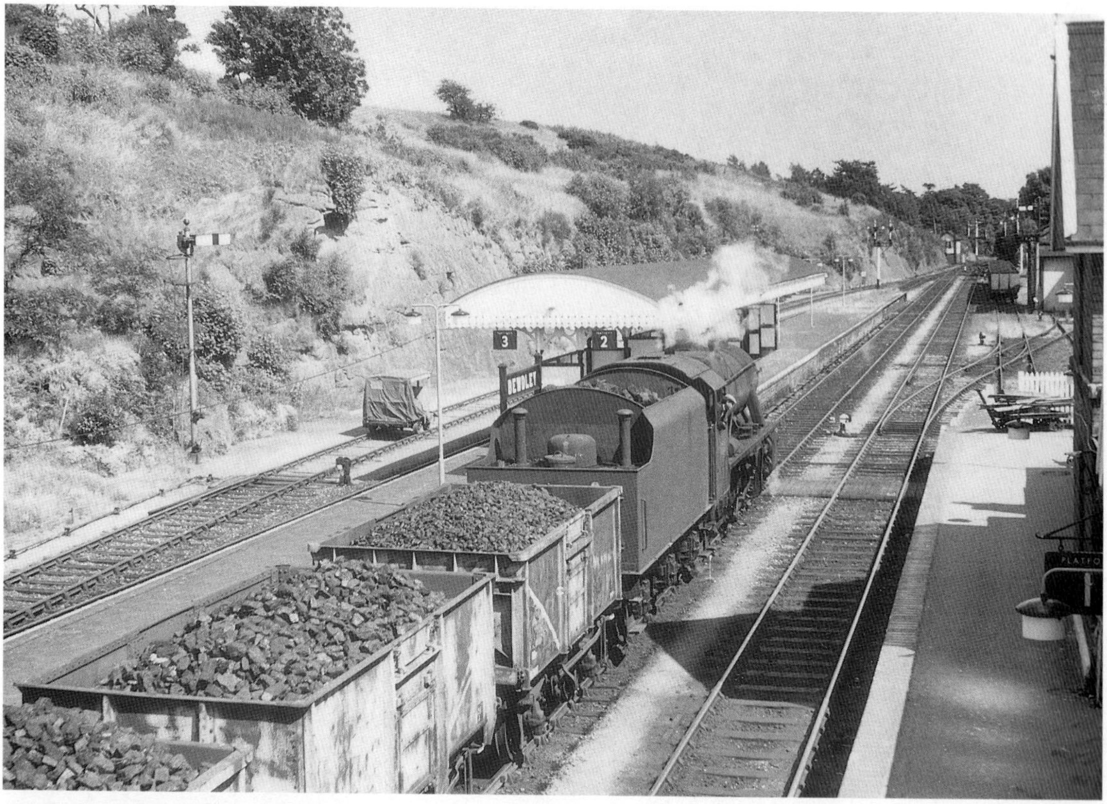
3
2
BEWDLEY

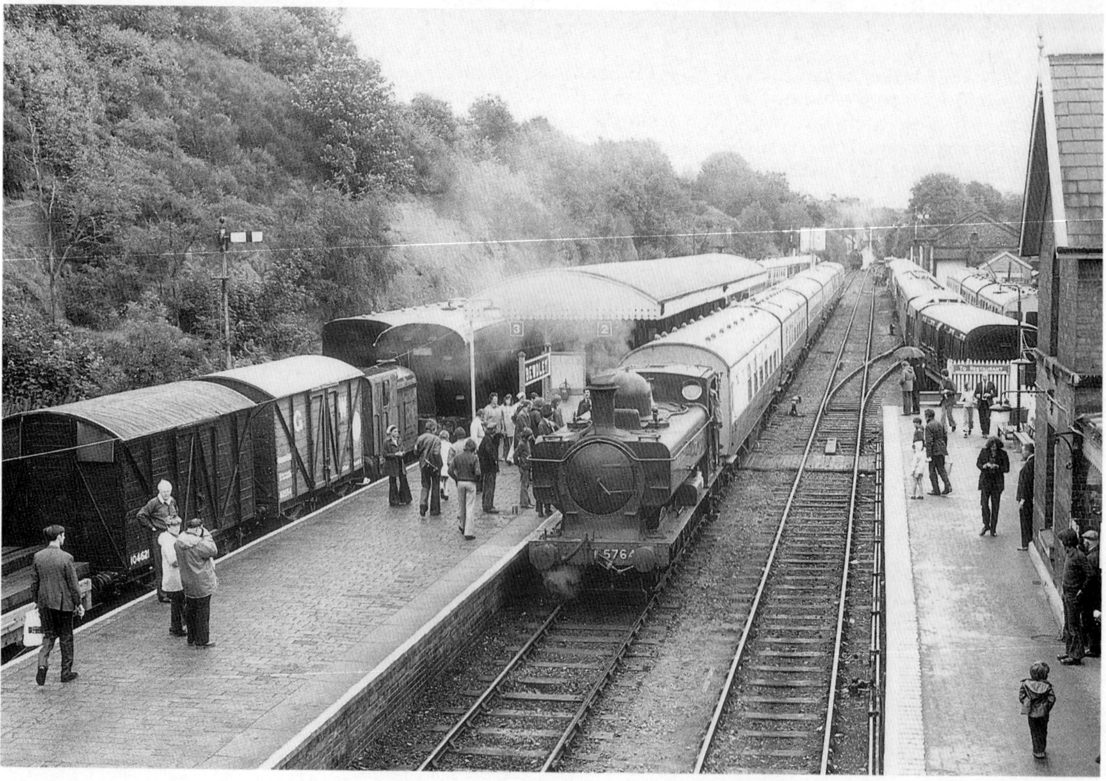
3
2
TO RESTAURANT

Still standing on the station footbridge but turning round to look the other way, we can see the whole of the Bewdley layout, looking towards Kidderminster and Stourport. The first picture is another of No 48531 heading through the station with the coal train for Stourport Power Station. Passenger trains southwards from Bewdley to Kidderminster and Hartlebury were still running at this time, and did so until January 1970.

The second view shows Bewdley station on 10 August 1974 (the first year of the SVR passenger service to Bewdley), with pannier tank No 5764 at platform 2 with a Bridgnorth train. Apart from the water tanks at the end of platforms 1 and 2, very little seems to have changed. All the signals are still there and Bewdley South signal box can be seen in the distance.

The third view of the station was taken on 1 August 1994, and shows '8F' No 48773 at platform 2 with the 2.15 pm Kidderminster to Bridgnorth train, while ex-GWR 2-8-0 No 2857 is in charge of the 1.30 pm Bridgnorth-Kidderminster service at platform 2, and empty stock occupies the other lines. What a busy scene this is compared to the first picture! There are now more railway signs, and the water tank at the end of platform 2 has been refurbished. *All RS*

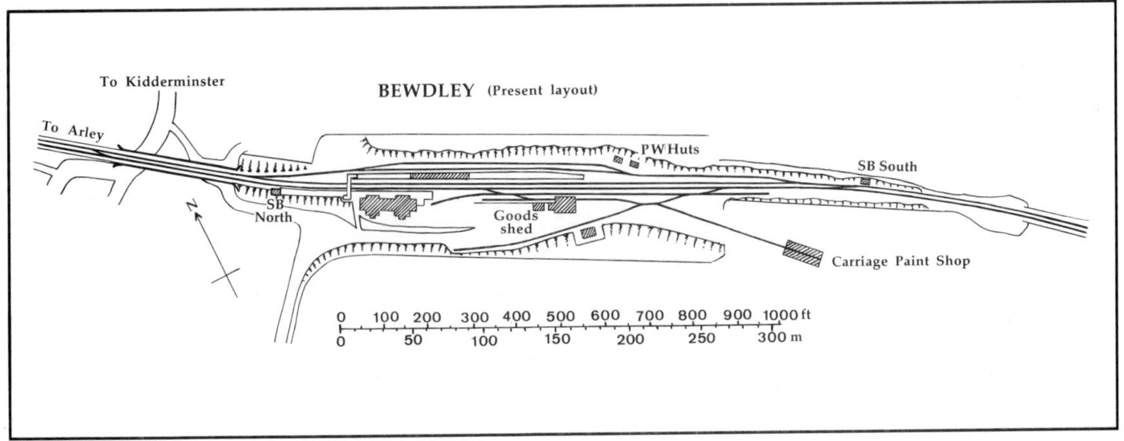

On 23 May 1966 ex-LMS '8F' No 48459 and brake-van are heading north from the Kidderminster direction tender-first for Highley, and are seen approaching Bewdley South signal box. Although the line appears to be double track leaving Bewdley, it is in fact two single lines, the nearer one being that to Stourport. Note the signalman by the box waiting to exchange tokens, and the junction crossover point for access to either line.

Very little seems to have changed in today's picture, taken on 29 July 1994, showing 2-6-0 No 46443 approaching Bewdley South box with the 2.15 pm Kidderminster-Bridgnorth service. Tokens are now exchanged at Bewdley North box. Although the crossover point is still in, the Stourport line is closed and has been lifted a few hundred yards south of here, the remaining part being used as a siding. The bracket signal is still there, plus an extra signal, and there is also a home and distant signal on the left-hand side of the tracks. *Both RS*

The '8F' and brake-van are seen again approaching Bewdley as they come off Sandbourne viaduct, just below Bewdley South box. This viaduct has ten arches and is 101 yards long. Just south of the viaduct a new Bewdley bypass was built in 1986, and at no cost to the SVR (unlike the Bridgnorth bypass) a new rail overbridge was built.

On 29 July 1994 No 46521 is about to cross Sandbourne viaduct with the 1.30 pm Bridgnorth-Kidderminster train. The only change in the pictures are the signals, which were installed in 1985. After crossing the viaduct the line passes over the new bypass, and just south of this the Kidderminster and Stourport lines diverged, the Kidderminster line swinging away to the east. *Both RS*

8
KIDDERMINSTER LOOP

Heading east from Bewdley, the Kidderminster line (known as the Kidderminster loop, the SVR proper running to Stourport and Hartlebury) passes the site of Rifle Range Halt. This was opened in 1905 and closed in 1920, used mainly by the TA to gain access to their training ground. Just after this the line enters Bewdley or Foley Park tunnel. In August 1959 ex-GWR Class '4MT' 2-6-2 tank No 5518 hurries out of the tunnel towards Bewdley with a local passenger train.

Thirty-five years later, on 28 August 1994, 2-6-0 No 46521 leaves the tunnel with the 3.45 pm Kidderminster-Bridgnorth train. Although No 46521 is an LMS-type locomotive, designed by Ivatt, it was actually built by British Railways at Swindon in 1953. *Brian Moone/RS*

Just south of Bewdley tunnel was Foley Park Halt, which opened in 1905 but closed in 1970 with the end of BR passenger services on the route. It was situated just under 2 miles from Kidderminster, halfway between there and Bewdley. On 9 August 1962 an unidentified Standard 2-6-2 tank pulls into the halt with a Bewdley-bound passenger train, which includes a fish van. Note the 'Pagoda'-type roof on the small waiting shelter, and also the sidings (looking disused) that served the sugar beet factory on the right, which BR continued to serve until 1980.

Today the sugar beet factory is still there, complete with huge silos, but the sidings have gone, although some of the trackbed remains. The high building on the right-hand side in the previous picture can just be seen above the trees in the 'present' view. The halt has completely disappeared, and will not be rebuilt because of problems with traffic on the nearby road bridge, which carries the busy A451 between Kidderminster and Stourport, and also lack of car-parking facilities in the area. On 26 August 1994 No 46521 hurries through the site of Foley Park Halt with the 13.30 Kidderminster-Bridgnorth train. *John Tennant/RS*

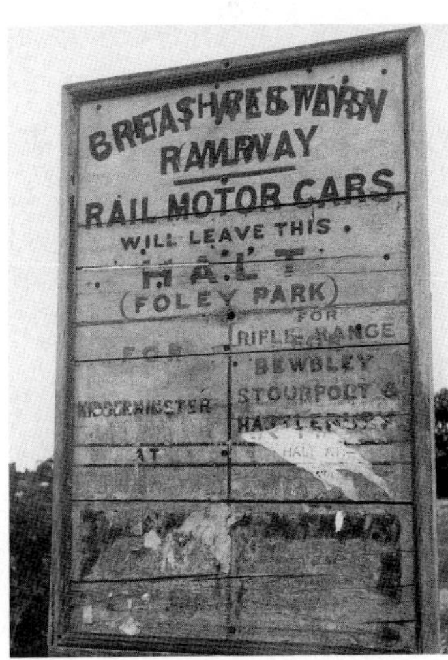

From GWR to BR(W) - an old notice at Foley Park Halt photographed in 1962. *John Tennant*

After leaving Foley Park and crossing over the seven-span Falling Sands viaduct that spans the River Stour and the Staffordshire & Worcestershire Canal, we approach Kidderminster and the junction of the SVR Bewdley to Kidderminster loop with the Birmingham to Worcester route. Situated on the south side of the SVR line at this point was Kidderminster locomotive shed (85D). On 10 November 1957 the late autumn sun highlights 0-6-0 pannier tank No 7700 as it rests outside the utilitarian-looking corrugated iron shed. This new locomotive shed was opened in 1932 to replace one nearer the station, and contained two roads. In its heyday there were 16 locomotives at 85D, including the CM&DPR pannier tanks Nos 28 and 29. The Severn Valley line can be seen at the right-hand edge of the picture.

Closure came in 1964 and the area where the shed stood is now a new housing estate, as this picture of the site taken on 23 September 1994 shows well. *Norman Glover/RS*

On 1 July 1961 Standard Class '3MT' 2-6-2 tank No 82032 with the 1.45 pm Shrewsbury-Kidderminster train joins the main Kidderminster-Worcester line at Kidderminster Junction, and heads north for the station. The line from Bewdley and Bridgnorth can be clearly seen on the right-hand side of the picture.

Today the junction between the SVR and BR lines is in the same position, but the line for the new SVR Kidderminster Town station, which was opened in 1984, now runs parallel with the BR route to the terminus. The new station was built on the site of the old Kidderminster goods yard, and is almost adjacent to the BR station. On 26 August 1994 Class '150' unit No 150123 passes Kidderminster Junction with the 14.28 Great Malvern-Birmingham New Street service. Some sidings have been removed and a new upper quadrant signal installed, but the signal box is still there. On the SVR side one can just see the fine new signal gantry that controls the Bewdley route from the new station. In the distance on the right-hand side, new houses and high-rise flats have been built. *Brian Moone/RS*

Ex-GWR '4MT' 2-6-2 tank No 6147 shunts in Kidderminster goods yard on 19 May 1965. The yard was closed 18 years later in May 1983, thus allowing the SVR to negotiate with BR for the extension of its line into Kidderminster. Up to that date the SVR owned the section from Bridgnorth to Foley Park, so it was allowed to purchase the 1 mile to Kidderminster Junction and lease the remaining quarter of a mile of the goods yard area. More recently the SVR has purchased this section.

Over the years the SVR has seen many famous locomotive visitors to the line, none more so than the ex-LNER 4-6-2 'Pacific' *Flying Scotsman*, originally No 4472, but now as it appeared in its last years of BR service (complete with German-type smoke deflectors) as No 60103. On 8 October 1994 No 60103 pulls out of Kidderminster Town station with the 1.00 pm to Bridgnorth. Note the splendid GWR-style signal box, erected by SVR staff and volunteers and opened in 1987. Some of the background buildings are still to be seen in the 'present' picture, but apart from that great changes have obviously taken place. *Brian Moone/RS*

Another view of the goods yard, this time also showing the southern exit from the BR station at Kidderminster. On 27 May 1961 ex-GWR 'Hall' Class 4-6-0 No 7910 *Hown Hall*, shedded at Southall (81C), passes a very busy-looking goods yard and heads south for Worcester with a mixed goods train. Kidderminster station is just visible to the right of the goods shed.

Passing the same spot over 33 years later, on 26 August 1994, is Class '150' unit No 150202 with the 11.01 Birmingham to Great Malvern service. Where the goods yard was is now the SVR station. The water tower and PW hut are still there, as is the large goods shed, which was purchased by the SVR in 1985 and is now used by the company's Carriage & Wagon Department. The bracket signal on the main line is still there, but is now upper quadrant. The change of style of signals in the area was due to the regional changes in the mid-'60s. Out of sight to the left of the picture, the SVR has just installed a 70-foot locomotive turntable, which used to be at Fort William. *Brian Moone/RS*

The Severn Valley Bewdley-Kidderminster loop originally finished at Kidderminster station on the Worcester-Stourbridge-Birmingham route (originally Snow Hill but now New Street station). On 9 April 1972 the 12.02 service from Kidderminster to Lichfield enters Kidderminster station, comprising a three-car Western suburban set and a three-car Metro Cammell set. In the background can be seen the northern end of the goods yard which in 1984 was transformed into the SVR's Kidderminster Town station and a vast car park to cater for the many thousands of visitors to the line each year.

The 'present' view shows Class '150' unit No 150120 entering the BR station with the 10.00 Hereford-Birmingham New Street service on 26 August 1994. The goods yard has now gone, to be replaced by the SVR car park and the new station, which consists of a double-faced island platform; both platforms have run-round facilities. The station building, off the right-hand side of the picture, is designed in a GWR style from the end of the last century (see page 78). *Michael Mensing/RS*

Ex-GWR railcar No 24 arrives at Kidderminster (BR) station on 30 August 1962 to form the 2.05 pm to Bridgnorth and Shrewsbury. Beyond the road overbridge can be seen a locomotive water tower set by the southbound loop line.

Both of these things have now gone in the picture of unit No 150002 as it draws into the refurbished station with the 13.33 Birmingham New Street-Great Malvern train on 26 August 1994. A 'bus shelter' has now replaced the GWR buildings and their lovely canopies, but the fine-looking house in the background appears unchanged. It is now obviously not possible to travel direct from this station to Shrewsbury; the service to Birmingham to the north and Worcester to the south is of a half-hour frequency. *Michael Mensing/RS*

Before leaving this section let's take a look at three Kidderminster stations. The first picture shows Kidderminster (BR) station in 1958, complete with elegant Elizabethan-style frontage. This station replaced the original, which was of wooden construction and was burned down.

Kidderminster station is seen as it is today in the second picture, taken on 2 September 1994. This functional-looking building replaced the previous station in the 1960s.

As if to complement the first picture, the final view shows the splendid-looking SVR Kidderminster Town station on 26 August 1994. This station, opened to the public in 1985, has many amenities for the general public. It incorporates a public house, appropriately called the 'King & Castle', and to the west side there is also a fine building housing a railway museum. Although almost adjacent to the BR station, the SVR station building is set at right angles to its neighbour. *R. S. Carpenter collection/RS (2)*

9
BEWDLEY TO WORCESTER

We now continue our journey on the Severn Valley 'main line' from south of Bewdley to Hartlebury and Worcester. Just over a mile from Bewdley station the line ran through the short Mount Pleasant tunnel, then a mile further on it ran into Burlish Halt, three-quarters of a mile to the north-west of Stourport station. Burlish Halt was opened in 1930 and was a typical GWR-style halt, complete with 'Pagoda'-roofed waiting shelter. On 27 June 1959 ex-GWR diesel railcar No W29 leaves Burlish Halt with the 4.25 pm from Hartlebury to Bewdley. The passenger service between those two places finished in January 1970 and the section of line from Bewdley South to Stourport closed at the same time.

Today, apart from the oak tree on the left-hand side, there is nothing at all left to tell us that Burlish Halt and the SVR existed in this location. The whole area is a vast housing estate, the only exception being the now privately owned crossing-keeper's cottage at the site of Burlish crossing, just over half a mile north-west of here, going towards Bewdley. *John Dew/RS*

Next we come to Stourport on Severn station. There were two through platforms at this station and a small goods yard and goods shed on the south side of the line. On the north side were sidings and a line running to a canal basin off the Staffordshire & Worcestershire Canal; there were sidings on both sides of the basin, plus another goods shed on the south side. The GWR brought coal, iron and steel to this basin to be shipped to the local ironworks at Wilden, situated a mile to the north-east of the station and right by the Stour. The barges using the S&W canal for part of the route then joined the River Stour for the rest of the journey. It might have been simpler to have built a short branch line to the works! In May 1963 ex-GWR 2-6-2 tank No 5153, having just taken water, leaves Stourport station with the daily pick-up freight from Hartlebury to Shrewsbury. Immediately on leaving the station the line crossed the busy A451 Kidderminster-Stourport road, the crossing gates for which can be seen in the bottom right-hand corner. Stourport, like its neighbour Bewdley, was and still is a favourite leisure resort with the people of Birmingham and the West Midlands; when the line was open, many excursions were run to both these riverside towns on Bank Holidays and in the summer months.

Looking at the scene today, it is impossible to tell that a station was here, but a resident of this road told me that on occasions he would find bits of track in his garden. Even the church (top right) has gone, only a few buttresses now remaining. *Brian Moone/RS*

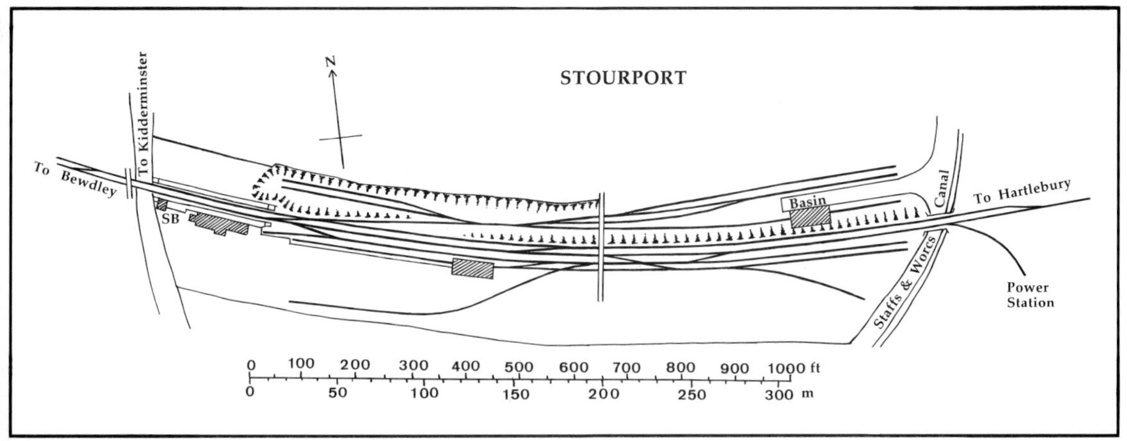

Some three-quarters of a mile east of Stourport station, after crossing over the S&W canal, a short branch line ran south to Stourport Power Station, a distance of just under a mile. BR locomotives were not allowed any further down the short branch than the Worcester road bridge, where there were exchange sidings, a few yards short of the Power Station. From this point onwards, and for shunting in the sidings in the Power Station, the CEGB at one time used a fleet of three 0-4-0 saddle tanks. There would normally be one or two locomotives in steam daily, with one spare or under repair. On 20 March 1972 *Sir Thomas Royden*, an outside-cylindered 0-4-0 saddle tank built by Andrew Barclay in 1940 (works No 2088), crosses the Worcester road bridge and heads for the Power Station with a load of coal from the interchange point. The last BR coal train ran in March 1979, and the track from the Power Station was lifted in 1983.

The plate girder bridge was dismantled in 1986, but one of the abutments still remains in this 5 August 1994 view. The 'Old Rose & Crown' has had a few minor modifications, including a new porch. The foreground roads now lead to a housing estate that was built when the Power Station was dismantled in the early 1980s. The Stourport to Worcester road used to pass under the line; this is the A4025, which joins the A449 trunk road from Kidderminster to Worcester at Crossway Green, 3 miles south-east of Stourport. *Both RS*

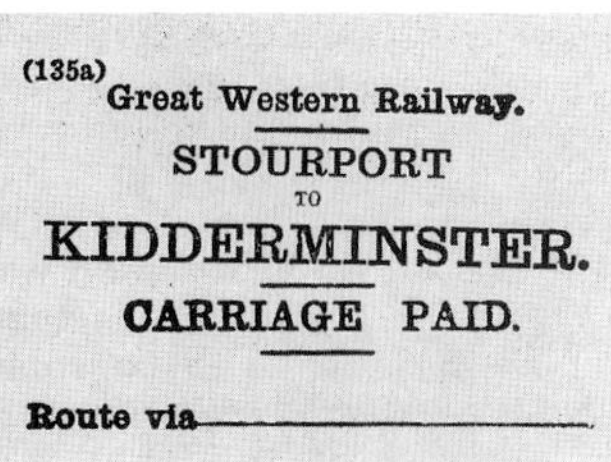

(135a)
Great Western Railway.

STOURPORT
TO
KIDDERMINSTER.
CARRIAGE PAID.

Route via__________

Once it leaves the canal and the riverside town of Stourport, the line runs due east for 2 miles through the pleasant Worcestershire countryside before swinging south to join the Kidderminster-Worcester line at Hartlebury Junction, half a mile north of the junction station. Two miles east of Stourport, near Park Farm, ex-GWR 2-6-2 tank No 5153 heads west with the 10.25 am Hartlebury-Shrewsbury goods on 1 June 1963.

After the line was dismantled in 1983, most of the trackbed of the line between Stourport and Hartlebury became the Leapgate Country Park walkway, including the section seen in the 'past' photograph. In the 'present' picture, taken in roughly the same spot, trees now hide the trackbed, and the pylon has been removed, but the distant tall fir tree on the right-hand horizon is still there as an identifying mark on 5 August 1994. *Brian Moone/RS*

On 21 July 1962 an ex-GWR Class '41xx' 2-6-2 tank enters Hartlebury with a Birmingham (Snow Hill) to Worcester train - note the station sign.

In today's scene, taken on 20 August 1994, Class '150' unit No 150010 enters Hartlebury with the 16.01 New Street-Great Malvern service. The signal box is still there, controlling the level crossing, but the footbridge has gone. Still dominating the scene is the high chimney of the Baggeridge Brick Company works, but the works buildings have been rebuilt. The small goods yards on either side of the line have now gone, but the crossover points connecting the up and down lines are still in place. The junction for the SVR line was 600 yards north of here, swinging away westwards towards Stourport. *R. Tennant/RS*

The next view at Hartlebury is taken from the southbound platform, and shows an ex-GWR diesel railcar with an afternoon service from Bewdley on 21 July 1962. This picture gives a good view of the old crossing gates and the buildings on the northbound platform. Look at the amount of parcels on that platform waiting to be loaded, probably on to a Snow Hill train. Note also the brick-built waiting room on the southbound platform, and the number of benches.

Hartlebury station buildings are now closed, and passengers joining trains here pay on the trains. On 20 August 1994 Class '150' unit No 150014 stops at the station with the 17.01 New Street to Great Malvern service. At the date of this picture only four trains each way stopped at this former junction station, two in the morning and two in the evening. The waiting room has been replaced, and so has the lighting, but the footbridge and benches have long gone. The buildings on the northbound platform are still there, but are no longer used by the railway, and a small 'bus shelter'-type of waiting room has been put on the platform to replace the old waiting room. *R. Tennant/RS*

The final picture at Hartlebury Junction shows the southern end of the station, again on 21 July 1962. The ex-GWR diesel railcar, seen in the previous 'past' picture, waits in the loop line as a Swindon 'Cross Country' DMU speeds through with a Cardiff-Birmingham Snow Hill train. The railcar will shortly be pulling into the northbound platform to form a return service to Bewdley. The short siding and platform on the right-hand side are for local coal traffic.

The scene on 13 August 1994, with Class '150' unit No 150011 forming the 15.03 Great Malvern-New Street service, shows how much railways have changed in the last 20 to 30 years. The signals have long gone and so have the sidings and loop lines. Where the coal siding and platform were has now been fenced off, and the land is part of a local factory. *R. Tennant/RS*

Although the original SVR line officially ends at Hartlebury Junction, we are carrying on to Worcester Shrub Hill, completing our journey from Shrewsbury to Worcester via the Oxford, Worcester & Wolverhampton Railway route.

The first station on the line to Worcester, some 3 miles south of Hartlebury, was Cutnall Green Halt, built to serve the small village of that name, a mile to the north-east of the station. As can be seen in this 1962 picture, looking north, the halt had two platforms complete with waiting shelters, and a siding leading to an MOD store, many of which were erected in this area during the last war. The GWR signal box completes the scene.

Today no trace of the halt exists, just the track of the Kidderminster-Worcester line. The date is 11 September 1994. *Lens of Sutton/RS*

Just under 6 miles south of Hartlebury is the important junction at Droitwich Spa. Here the ex-GWR line from Birmingham Snow Hill to Worcester meets the former LMS loop line to Worcester. The latter line leaves the Birmingham-Bristol main line at Stoke Works Junction, south of Bromsgrove, and rejoins the route at Abbotswood Junction, 4 miles south of Worcester. On 1 July 1983 Class '37' No 37224 shunts in the coal sidings just north of Droitwich station. This view clearly shows the junction, with the Kidderminster line swinging away to the left and the Bromsgrove route to the right. The GWR signal box is situated in the apex of the junction, and lower-quadrant signals abound.

Some 11 years later, on 13 August 1994, Class '150' unit No 150011 approaches Droitwich Spa station with the 13.31 New Street-Great Malvern (via Kidderminster) service. Most of the Birmingham-Worcester trains now travel via Kidderminster, the Worcester-Bromsgrove route seeing only a limited service. The signal box and semaphores are still in place, but although the coal yard is still there, the coal sidings and thus the connection with BR have disappeared. *Both RS*

A view of Droitwich Spa station in 1962, looking south. This spa town is famous for its salt baths, among other things, and was much featured in pre-war GWR publicity posters.

The second view, taken on 11 September 1994, shows the refurbished station. The footbridge is still there, although without its roof, a common practice nowadays. The buildings on the northbound platform have gone and been replaced with 'bus shelters'. However, some of the buildings remain on the southbound platform - there is still a booking office - although the elegant GWR canopy has gone. The roadbridge is part of the new link road between the town and the bypass (situated to the west and north of the town). *Lens of Sutton/RS*

The only station on the 5½ miles between Droitwich and Worcester was Fernhill Heath, some 3 miles south of Droitwich. This view of Fernhill Heath station, looking north, was taken in 1962, showing the buildings on the northbound platform and the signal box at the end of it. Fernhill Heath, like Cutnall Green, was never a very busy station (certainly not in post-war years), both only having a sparse passenger service with perhaps a daily quota of four trains each way, usually morning and evening. I remember this route very well, being stationed at Worcester in National Service days, and travelling regularly by both routes to the Birmingham area; but only on very rare occasions do I remembers the train stopping at Fernhill Heath (or at Cutnall Green), unlike Hartlebury, where the trains always stopped and cry was 'Hartlebury, change for Bewdley and Bridgnorth'.

In today's picture of Fernhill Heath, taken on 12 September 1994, only the curve of the track and the land on the left-hand side give any identification with the 'past' picture. *Lens of Sutton/RS*

10
WORCESTER

After passing through Rainbow Hill tunnel the line comes to Worcester Tunnel Junction, where the Shrub Hill and Foregate Street (for Hereford) lines divide. On 19 April 1962 ex-GWR 2-6-2 tank No 4111 is seen passing the junction signal box heading for Foregate Street station with the 4.25 pm Birmingham Snow Hill to Great Malvern train. In the background is the enormous goods yard, goods shed and also the works. At the top right-hand edge of the picture is part of one of the locomotive sheds, there being two at Worcester (85A) set in the triangle of the Shrub Hill and Foregate Street lines. In its heyday, Worcester was truly a great railway centre.

On 31 July 1994 a Class '150' unit heads for Worcester Shrub Hill station with the 16.30 service from Stratford upon Avon to Hereford. When it arrives at Shrub Hill the driver will change ends and the unit will head down the bank to Foregate Street and Hereford. The junction signal box and signals remain, but everything else has virtually disappeared, only the trackbed of the sidings remaining. *Michael Mensing/RS*

This is the view from the platform at Shrub Hill station, looking north on the evening of 24 June 1973, as ex-GWR 'Hall' Class 4-6-0 No 6998 *Burton Agnes Hall* struggles up the steep bank from Foregate Street station with a return special from Hereford to Didcot. The smaller of the two locomotive sheds can be seen with a Hymek diesel-hydraulic locomotive standing outside. These short-lived locomotives were regular performers on the Worcester-Hereford service in the 1960s and early 1970s. The roof of the other shed can just be seen above the 'Hall'.

Today's view shows many changes, as 'Turbo' unit No 166211 approaches Shrub Hill station with the (SuO) 19.32 Great Malvern to Paddington service on 31 July 1994. The locomotive sheds have gone (they disappeared in the late 1980s), leaving sidings with overhead lights for the stabling various DMUs. The splendid bracket signal is still there, but it has been moved nearer to the station, and the signal box that was in the 'V' of the triangle has long since gone, together with some signals. The sidings on the left-hand side have been taken up, and some by the site of the shed, and there are now more signs on or by the foot crossing, and the lighting has been changed. *Both RS*

The final picture shows ex-GWR 'Hall' Class 4-6-0 No 6992 ***Arborfield Hall*** waiting to leave Shrub Hill on Sunday 30 March 1958 with the 10.00 am Paddington-Hereford train, the 'Hall' having just taken over for this final section.

It is not often that you can copy yesterday's pictures with steam power, but on Sunday 11 September 1994 'Britannia' 'Pacific' No 70000 obliged the author by pulling into the same spot as in the previous picture, as it left Shrub Hill station with the empty coaching stock of a special train that it had brought in from Didcot. Some of the background buildings remain, but the two archways on the left have gone and there are now three lines in the station (only two through lines) compared to the four of yesteryear. *Michael Mensing/RS*

TIMETABLES FOR THE SEVERN VALLEY LINE BETWEEN WORCESTER AND SHREWSBURY, 13 JUNE-11 SEPTEMBER 1960

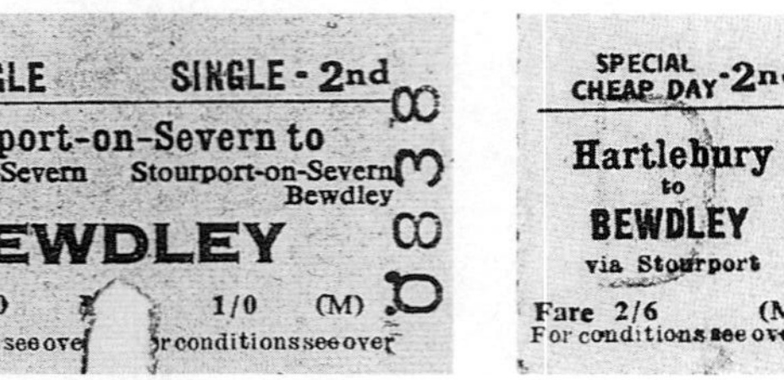

Table 176

Table 176 WORCESTER, HARTLEBURY, KIDDERMINSTER, BEWDLEY, TENBURY WELLS, WOOFFERTON, BRIDGNORTH and SHREWSBURY

WEEK DAYS (for Sunday service, see page 527)

Miles from Hartlebury	Miles from Kidderm'ter		am (2)	am	am	am	am (2)	am	am	am	am	am	am	am	am	am	am	am	am	pm (2)	pm	pm
		164 Worcester (Shrub H) dp			6 25		6 55		7F44		8F28	8F 7		9F50	1015			10 15	11F 3		12 24	
		179 Birmingham (S.H.) "		5 45							8 0		8 48	10 0				10 0	11 0		12 0	
		179 Stourbridge Jn. "		6 35	(2)				(2)		8 32	(2)	9 37	1024	1037			10 37	11 37		12 37	
—	—	Hartlebury dep			7 0		7 17		8 10			9 30								12 8		
2¾	—	Stourport-on-Severn			7 8		7 24		8 17			9 38								1214		
3½		Burlish Halt			7 10		7 26		8 19		(2)	9 40					(2)	(2)		1217		(2)
—	—	Kidderminster ¶ dep	5 45	7 0							8 55		10 2	1040	1052			11 0	11 52		12 51	
—	1¼	Foley Park Halt	5 49	7 4							8 59		10 6	1044	1056			11 4	11 56		12 55	
5½	3½	Bewdley arr	5 54	7 9	7 15		7 31		8 24		9 4	9 45	1012	1049	11 2			11 9	12 2	1222	1 0	
		Bewdley dep	5 55		7 16				8 35		9 5			1050			11 10	11 10				1 7
10	8	Wyre Forest									9 15						11 20	11 20				
12	10	Cleobury Mortimer									9 21						11 26	11 26				
15½	13½	Neen Sollars									9 28						11 33	11 33				
17½	15½	Newnham Bridge									9 34						11 39	11 39				
21	19	Tenbury Wells arr						(2)		(2)	9 40						11 45	11 45				
		Tenbury Wells dep						7 55		8 50							11 48	11 48				
23½	21½	Easton Court A						8 0		8 55							11 53	11 53				
26	24	Woofferton arr						8 5		9 0							11 58	11 58				
—	28½	164 Ludlow arr						8 20									12 49	12 49				
—	30½	164 Leominster "								9 13												
7½	5½	Northwood Halt dep	5 58		7 19				8 38					1053								1 10
9½	7½	Arley	6 4		7 25				8 43					1059								1 16
11½	9½	Highley	6 11		7 32				8 50					11 6								1 23
13¾	11¾	Hampton Loade			7 39				8 57					1112								
16	14	Eardington Halt			7 45				9 3					1118								
18¼	16¼	Bridgnorth arr			7 49				9 9					1122								
		Bridgnorth dep				7 57										1130						
22½	20½	Linley Halt				8 5										1138						
25½	23½	Coalport				8 10										1145						
25¾	23¾	Jackfield Halt				8 13										1149						
27½	25½	Iron Bridge and Broseley				8 17										1155						
28½	26½	Buildwas				8 22										12 1						
32½	30½	Cressage				8 30										1210						
33¾	31¾	Cound Halt				8 34										1215						
36½	34½	Berrington				8 41										1222						
40¾	38¾	Shrewsbury arr				8 52										1236						
												Saturdays only	Saturdays only	Saturdays only	Saturdays only	Saturdays only	Saturdays only	Except Saturdays	Saturdays only	Saturdays only	Saturdays only	Saturdays only

WEEK DAYS—*continued*

	pm (2)		pm	pm	pm	pm	pm	pm	pm (2)	pm	pm (2)	pm	pm	pm (2)	pm	pm	pm	pm	pm	pm	pm	pm	pm
164 Worcester (Shrub H) dp	1 45			1N30		1F36		3F10		3 30		3 30		4F 5			5F25		5F25	6 20	6 20		7F49
179 Birmingham (S.H.) "			1245	1 0		1 15	2 0	3 0		3 0					5 0				5 40	6 0	6 15		8 8
179 Stourbridge Jn. "			1 22	1 37		1 52	2 37	3 37		3B37					5 24	(2)	(2)		6 5	6 37	6 52		8 45
Hartlebury dep	2 3											4 15		4 25		5 30	6 8						
Stourport-on-Severn	2 10											4 21		4 33		5 42	6 16						
Burlish Halt	2 12		(2)	(2)	(2)					(2)		4 23		4 35		5 45	6 18		(2)			(2)	
Kidderminster ¶ dep			2 5	2 5		2 14	2 52	3 52		4 10			4 22		5 41				6 22	6 52	7 9		9 0
Foley Park Halt			2 9	2 9		2 18	2 56	3 56		4 14			4 26		5 45				6 26	6 56	7 13		9 4
Bewdley arr	2 18		2 14	2 14		2 23	3 2	4 2		4 19		4 29	4 32	4 42	5 50	5 51	6 23		6 32	7 2	7 18		9 10
Bewdley dep			2 20	2 20	2 21					4 20			4 35			6 0	6 38		6 33			7 26	
Wyre Forest					2 32					4 30									6 43				
Cleobury Mortimer					2 37					4 36									6 49				
Neen Sollars					2 44					4 42									6 57				
Newnham Bridge					2 48					4 47									7 3				
Tenbury Wells arr					2 55					4 53									7 10				
Tenbury Wells dep									4 46		5 40								7 12				
Easton Court A									4 51		5 45								7 16				
Woofferton arr									4 56		5 50								7 21				
164 Ludlow arr									5 18		6 1								8 40				
164 Leominster "									5 31		7 2								7 37				
Northwood Halt dep			2 24	2 24									4 41			6 4	6 42					7 29	
Arley			2 29	2 29									4 46			6 9	6 47					7 34	
Highley			2 35	2 35									4 53			6 15	6 53					7 40	
Hampton Loade			2 43	2 43									5 0			6 20							
Eardington Halt			2 48	2 48									5 6			6 25							
Bridgnorth arr			2 53	2 53									5 12			6 30							
Bridgnorth dep			2 54	2 54									5 25					7 32					
Linley Halt			3 1	3 1									5 33					7 40					
Coalport			3 7	3 7									5 37					7 46					
Jackfield Halt			3 11	3 11									5 41					7 50					
Iron Bridge and Broseley			3 16	3 16									5 48					7 56					
Buildwas			3 22	3 22									66 3					8 0					
Cressage			3 29	3 29									6 12					8 7					
Cound Halt			3 34	3 34									6 15					8 11					
Berrington			3 41	3 41									6 23					8 17					
Shrewsbury arr			3 54	3 54									6 37					8 31					
	Saturdays only. TC Worcester to Tenbury Wells. For continuation see Bewdley dep 2 21 pm		Saturdays only	Except Saturdays	Saturdays only	Saturdays only	Saturdays only	Saturdays only				Saturdays only		Except Saturdays						Saturdays only	Except Saturdays		Saturdays only

A Station for Little Hereford (½ mile)
B Except Saturdays depart 3 47 pm
F Foregate Street station
6 Arr 5 53 pm
N Second class only
p pm
TC Through Carriages
(2) Second class only

¶ A Road Service is operated between the Railway Station and the centre of the town by the Birmingham and Midland Motor Omnibus Co. Ltd. For particulars, see local announcements

525

Table 176—*continued* SHREWSBURY, BRIDGNORTH, WOOFFERTON, TENBURY WELLS, BEWDLEY, KIDDERMINSTER, HARTLEBURY and WORCESTER

WEEK DAYS (for Sunday service see page 527)

	Mile	Miles from Woofferton	am	am ②	am ②	am	am ②	am ②	am ②	am ②	am ②	am ②	am ②	am	am ②	am ②	am	am ②	am	pm	pm	am ②
														Saturdays only	Except Saturdays	Saturdays only	Saturdays only	Saturdays only	Saturdays only	Saturdays only	Saturdays only	Except Saturdays
Shrewsbury .. .. dep	—					6 40								9 50								
Berrington	4¼					6 50								10 0								
Cound Halt	7													10 6								
Cressage	8½					7 0								1011								
Buildwas	12½					7 8								1020								
Iron Bridge and Broseley	13½					7 14								1026								
Jackfield Halt	15					7 19								1031								
Coalport	15½					7 24								1036								
Linley Halt	18½					7 30								1042								
Bridgnorth arr	22½					7 38								1049								
Bridgnorth dep											8 0		9 20								1210	
Eardington Halt	24¾					Stop					8 5		9 25								1215	
Hampton Loade	27				6 50						8 11		9 31								1221	
Highley	29½				6 57						8 16		9 36								1231	
Arley	31½		5 45	6 30	7 4						8 23		9 44								1238	
Northwood Halt	33½		5 50	6 35	7 9						8 28		9 48								1243	
164Leominster .. dep	—							6 45														
164Ludlow	—							7 22				8 22										1127
Woofferton .. .. dep	—	—						7 35				8 33										1210
Easton Court A	—	2½						7 41				8 38										1215
Tenbury Wells arr	—	5						7 45				8 42										1219
Tenbury Wells dep										7 55					9 50	9 50						1220
Newnham Bridge	—	8½								8 3					9 58	9 58						1228
Neen Sollars	—	10½								8 8					10 3	10 3						1233
Cleobury Mortimer	—	14								8 20					10 10	1010						1240
Wyre Forest	—	16								8 25					10 15	1015						1245
Bewdley arr	35½	20½	5 53	6 38	7 13	am				8 34	8 32		9 52		10 22	1022					1247	1252
Bewdley dep			5 59	6 39		7 26	7 37		7 54	8 35	8 38		9 53		10 23		1030	10 35	11 30	1230	1249	1253
Foley Park Halt	37¼	22½	6 5			7 31			7 59	8 40			9 58		10 28		1035		11 35	1235		1258
Kidderminster ¶ .. arr	38¾	24	6 10			7 35			8 3	8 44			10 2		10 36		1040		11 40	1240		1 2
Burlish Halt .. .. dep	37¼	22¼		6 43			7 42				8 43							10 40			1254	
Stourport-on-Severn	38	23¼		6 46			7 45				8 46							10 43			1258	
Hartlebury .. .. arr	40¾	26		6 53			7 52				8 52							10 50			1 4	
179Stourbridge Jn. .. arr	—	30¾	6 26			7 53			8‡28	9‡ 1			10H32		10‡56		1056		11 56	1256		1‡34
179Birmingham (S.H.) „	57¾	42¾	7 5			8 33			9‡ 1	9‡30			10H55		11‡33		1133		12 31	1 31		2‡ 1
164Worcester(ShrubH) „	52	37½		7B48		8F31	8B31		8‡42	9‡58	9G18		10B56		11‡54		1154	11‡54	12H33	1 42	1 42	1B56

WEEK DAYS—*continued*

	am ②	pm	pm ②	pm	pm		pm	pm ②	pm	pm ②		pm ②	pm ②	pm ②	pm	pm	pm ②	pm ②	pm	pm ②	pm ②	pm ②	pm
	Saturdays only	Saturdays only	Saturdays only	Saturdays only	Saturdays only			Saturdays only	Saturdays only														Saturdays only
Shrewsbury .. .. dep							1 45							4 20		5 28							
Berrington							1 55							4 30		5 41							
Cound Halt							2 0							4 36		5 47							
Cressage							2 5							4 41		5 52							
Buildwas							2 15							4c51		6c 3							
Iron Bridge and Broseley							2 21							4 56		6 9							
Jackfield Halt							2 25							5 1		6 14							
Coalport							2 30							5 5		6 19							
Linley Halt							2 36							5 11		6 25							
Bridgnorth arr							2 44							5 18		6 33							
Bridgnorth dep							3 4							5 20								7 55	
Eardington Halt							3 9							5 25								8 0	
Hampton Loade							3 16							5 32								8 7	
Highley			1 30				3 24							5 40				7 0		7 50		8 12	
Arley			1 37				3 31							5 47				7 6		7 57		8 19	
Northwood Halt			1 42				3 36							5 52				7 11		8 2		8 24	
164Leominster .. dep												3 50					5 1						
164Ludlow „	1115											4 15					5 14				7 20		
Woofferton .. .. dep	1210											4 30					5 25				7 38		
Easton Court A	1215											4 36					5 31				7 43		
Tenbury Wells arr	1219											4 40					5 35				7 48		
Tenbury Wells dep	1220							3 5					4 58								7 49		
Newnham Bridge	1228							3 12					5 6								7 56		
Neen Sollars	1233							3 18					5 12								8 2		
Cleobury Mortimer	1240							3 24					5 19								8 8		
Wyre Forest	1245							3 29					5 24								8 13		
Bewdley arr	1253		1 47				3 40	3 38					5 32	5 55				7 16		8 6	8 21	8 27	
Bewdley dep	1 2	1 30	1 48	2 30	3 30		3 42	3 44	4 39	4 50			5 33	5 56	6 34				7 30	8 7		8 30	9 30
Foley Park Halt	1 7	1 35		2 35	3 35		3 47		4 44					6 2	6 38				7 35			8 35	9 35
Kidderminster ¶ .. arr	1 11	1 40		2 40	3 40		3 51		4 49					6 6	6 42				7 40			8 41	9 40
Burlish Halt .. .. dep			1 53					3 49		4 55			5 37							8 12			
Stourport-on-Severn			1 57					3 52		4 58			5 41							8C25			
Hartlebury .. .. arr			2 3					3 59		5 4			5 48							8 32			
179Stourbridge Jn. .. arr	1‡56	1 56		2 56	3 56		4 26		5 9						6 58				7 56			8 52	9 56
179Birmingham (S.H.) „	2‡31	2 31		3 31	4 31		5 47		5 47						7 33				8 31			9‡31	1031
164Worcester(ShrubH) „	1‡42		2F26				5F 5	5B 5	5 41	5‡41			6‡25	6B40					8F21	8 53		9 56	1038

A Station for Little Hereford (½ mile)
B Foregate St station, First & Second class
C Arr 8 15 pm
c Arr 3 minutes *earlier*
F Foregate Street station
G On Saturdays arr 9‡58 am
H On Saturdays arr Stourbridge Jn. 10‡26 am, Birmingham (S.H.) 11‡0 am
‖ Second class only
TC Through Carriages
② Second class only
‡ First and Second class

¶ A Road Service is operated between the Railway Station and the centre of the town by the Birmingham and Midland Motor Omnibus Co. Ltd. For particulars, see local announcements

Table 176—*continued* WORCESTER, HARTLEBURY, KIDDERMINSTER, BEWDLEY, TENBURY WELLS, WOOFFERTON, BRIDGNORTH and SHREWSBURY

SUNDAYS

	am	am	am	am	am	am	am		am	pm	pm	pm	pm	pm		pm	pm	pm	pm	pm	pm	pm
		TC to Stourport-on-Severn	TC to Birmingham (S.H.)			TC to Birmingham (S.H.)			TC to Stourport-on-Severn	TC to Birmingham (S.H.)		TC to Stourport-on-Severn	TC to Birmingham (S.H.)			TC to Stourport-on-Severn		TC to Birmingham (S.H.)		TC to Stourport-on-Severn	TC to Birmingham (S.H.)	
164Worcester(ShrubH) dp					10F23				11F56			1 45				4F 7						6F59
179Birmingham (S.H.) „	7 30	8 5		8 55	9 55		1055		11 55		1255	1 55		2 55		3 55	4 25		4 55	5 55		6 55
179Stourbridge Jn. „	8 12	8 45		9 35	10 35		1135		12p35		1 35	2 35		3 35		4 35	4 53		5 35	6 35		7 35
Hartlebury .. .. dep																						
Stourport-on-Severn			9 40			1140				1 40			3 40					5 40			7 40	
Burlish Halt																						
Kidderminster ¶ .. dep	8 22	9 1		9 45	11 5		1145		12 45		1 45	2 46		3 46		4 46	5 32		5 46	6 46		7 46
Foley Park Halt																						
Bewdley arr	8 30	9 10	9 46	9 53	11 13	1146	1153		12 53	1 46	1 53	2 54	3 46	3 54		4 54	5 40	5 46	5 54	6 54	7 46	7 54
Bewdley dep	8 33			9 56			1156				1 56			3 56			5 42		5 56			7 56
Wyre Forest																						
Cleobury Mortimer																						
Neen Sollars																						
Newnham Bridge																						
Tenbury Wells arr																						
Tenbury Wells dep																						
Easton Court A																						
Woofferton arr																						
164Ludlow .. .. arr																						
164Leominster „							noon															
Northwood Halt .. dep	8 40			10 0			12 0				2 0			4 0			5 45		6 0			8 0
Arley	8 48			10 6			12 6				2 6			4 6			5 52		6 6			8 6
Highley	8 56										2 14						5 59					8 14
Hampton Loade	9 4										2 19						6 5					8 19
Eardington Halt	9 10																					
Bridgnorth arr	9 15																6 15					
Bridgnorth dep																						
Linley Halt																						
Coalport																						
Jackfield Halt																						
Iron Bridge and Broseley																						
Buildwas																						
Cressage																						
Cound Halt																						
Berrington																						
Shrewsbury arr																						

SUNDAYS

	am	am	am	am	am	am		pm	pm	pm	pm	pm	pm	pm	pm		pm	pm	pm	pm	pm	pm
	TC from Birmingham (S.H.)		TC from Stourport-on-Severn			TC from Stourport-on-Severn			TC from Birmingham (S.H.)	TC from Stourport-on-Severn		TC from Birmingham (S.H.)	TC from Stourport-on-Severn		TC from Birmingham (S.H.)		TC from Stourport-on-Severn		TC from Birmingham (S.H.)		TC from Stourport-on-Severn	
Shrewsbury .. .. dep																						
Berrington																						
Cound Halt																						
Cressage																						
Buildwas																						
Iron Bridge and Broseley																						
Jackfield Halt																						
Coalport																						
Linley Halt																						
Bridgnorth arr																						
Bridgnorth dep		9 20																		6 48		
Eardington Halt																				6 52		
Hampton Loade		9 29									2 30									6 59		8 30
Highley		9 35									2 36									7 6		8 36
Arley		9 42		1045				1245			2 45			4 45				6 45		7 15		8 45
Northwood Halt		9 47		1051				1251			2 51			4 51				6 51		7 21		8 51
164Leominster .. dep																						
164Ludlow „																						
Woofferton .. .. dep																						
Easton Court A																						
Tenbury Wells arr																						
Tenbury Wells dep																						
Newnham Bridge																						
Neen Sollars																						
Cleobury Mortimer																						
Wyre Forest																						
Bewdley arr		9 50		1054				1254			2 54			4 54				6 54		7 24		8 54
Bewdley dep	9 14		9 56	1056	1118	11 56		1256	1258	1 56	2 56	2 59	3 56	4 56	4 59		5 56	6 56	6 59	7 26	7 56	8 56
Foley Park Halt																						
Kidderminster ¶ .. arr			10 7	11 5		12 5		1 5		2 5	3 5		4 5	5 5			6 5	7 5		7 35	8 5	9 5
Burlish Halt .. .. dep																						
Stourport-on-Severn	9 21				1124				1 4			3 5			5 5				7 5			
Hartlebury .. .. arr																						
179Stourbridge Jn. .. arr			10 18	1118		12 18		1 18		2 18	3 18		4 18	5 18			6 18	7 18		7 48	8 18	9 18
179Birmingham (S.H.) „			10 54	1154		12 54		1 54		2 54	3 54		4 54	5 54			6 54	7 54		8 26	8 54	9 54
164Worcester(ShrubH) „			11F13			12F44					3F39		5F25	6 27			6F37			8F28	9 12	10F39

For Notes, see pages 525 and 526

INDEX OF LOCATIONS